NOBEL PRIZE-WINNING

SCIENTISTS

MARIE CURIE

PIONEER ON THE FRONTIER OF RADIOACTIVITY

Judy L. Hasday

Enslow Publishers, Inc.

40 Industrial Road	PO Box 38
Box 398	Aldershot
Berkeley Heights, NJ 07922	Hants GU12 6BP
USA	UK

http://www.enslow.com

"Thanks to this discovery of new, very powerful radioactive substances, particularly radium, the study of radioactivity progressed. . . . it was obvious that a new science was in course of development."

—Marie Curie

In memory of Barbara Jean Hasday, a loving, compassionate, and deeply committed human being. A light went out with your passing; you will be profoundly missed by those whose life you so blessed with your own.

Library of Congress Cataloging-in-Publication Data

Hasday, Judy L., 1957–
    Marie Curie : pioneer on the frontier of radioactivity / Judy L. Hasday.
        p. cm. — (Nobel Prize-winning scientists)
    Includes bibliographical references and index.
    ISBN 0-7660-2440-7
    1. Curie, Marie, 1867–1934. 2. Women chemists—Poland—Biography.
I. Title. II. Series.
QD22.C8H29 2004
540'.92—dc22

                                2004001734

Printed in the United States of America

10 9 8 7 6 5 4 3 2 1

To Our Readers:
We have done our best to make sure all Internet Addresses in this book were active and appropriate when we went to press. However, the author and the publisher have no control over and assume no liability for the material available on those Internet sites or on other Web sites they may link to. Any comments or suggestions can be sent by e-mail to comments@enslow.com or to the address on the back cover.

Every effort has been made to locate all copyright holders of material used in this book. If any errors or omissions have occurred, corrections will be made in future editions of this book.

Illustration Credits: © The Nobel Foundation, p. 5; Archiv Pierre et Marie Curie, pp. 11, 18, 40, 44, 57, 66, 69, 83; ArtToday.com, pp. 53, 74; Enslow Publishers, Inc., pp. 16, 48, 87; Pressens Bild, p. 94.

Cover Illustration: Archiv Pierre et Marie Curie (foreground); © Photodisk, Inc. (background).

CONTENTS

THE NOBEL PRIZE

Every year since its founding in 1901, the Nobel Prize has been awarded to individuals who have distinguished themselves in the fields of physiology or medicine, physics, chemistry, literature, and peace. (In 1969 a prize for economics was added.) The prize is named for Alfred Nobel, a Swede born in Stockholm in 1833, who grew up to become a successful chemist, manufacturer, and businessman.

Nobel began experimenting with ways to make nitroglycerine safer for practical use. Eventually he found a way to mix nitroglycerine with silica and make a paste. He could then shape the paste into a stick that could be placed in holes drilled in rocks. He patented this creation in 1867 and named it dynamite. In order to detonate the dynamite sticks, Nobel also invented a blasting cap that could be ignited by burning a fuse. The invention of dynamite, along with equipment like the diamond drilling crown and the pneumatic drill, significantly reduced the expenses associated with many types of construction work.

Soon Nobel's dynamite and blasting caps were in great demand. Nobel proved to be an astute businessman, establishing companies and laboratories throughout the world. He also continued to experiment with other chemical inventions and held more than 350 patents in his lifetime.

Alfred Nobel did not narrow his learning just to scientific knowledge. His love of literature and poetry prompted him to write his own works, and his social conscience kept him interested in peace-related issues.

When Nobel died on December 10, 1896, and his will was read, everyone was surprised to learn that he left instructions that the accumulated fortune from his companies and business ventures (estimated at more than $3 million U.S.) was to be used to award prizes in physics, chemistry, physiology or medicine, literature, and peace.

In fulfilling Alfred Nobel's will, the Nobel Foundation was established in order to oversee the funds left by Nobel and to coordinate the work of the prize-awarding institutions. Nobel prizes are presented every December 10, the anniversary of Alfred Nobel's death.

A First for the Nobel Academy

The 1911 Nobel Prize in Chemistry was awarded amid a whirl of controversy surrounding the announcement of its latest recipient, Marie Curie. Usually, any of the prestigious awards in the categories of chemistry, physics, physiology/medicine, literature, peace, and economics (added in 1969) are an honor worthy of worldwide recognition and praise. At the time Marie Curie received the telegram on November 7, 1911, from the Academy of Sciences members in Stockholm informing her of her selection as the recipient of the award in chemistry, she had already been the subject of much discussion in the press. As her daughter Eve Curie would later write in her biography of her mother: "A great discovery, universal celebrity, and two Nobel prizes had fixed the admiration of a great many contemporaries upon Marie—and therefore the animosity of a great many others. Malice burst upon her in a sudden squall and attempted to annihilate her."[1]

At age forty-four, a fragile, weary, and very alone Marie Curie was being crushed by the scrutiny imposed on her by both jealous detractors and high-minded members of society. Instead of lauding Curie's achievements and admiring her devotion to her beloved profession, she was being reviled over an alleged affair with French physicist Paul Langevin. Though Curie had maintained a quiet, dignified widow's life after the devastating loss of her husband and scientific collaborator Pierre five years earlier, most colleagues and headline-hungry newspapers seemed more intent on portraying her as a home wrecker who now dishonored a name long recognized for brilliance in science.

Colleague Paul Langevin, a former student of Pierre Curie, had been a great admirer of Marie's husband. While studying and working with Pierre, Langevin developed a friendship with both Curies and a great admiration for their scientific endeavors. After Pierre's death, Langevin and Marie remained close friends. Langevin was married with four children. However, it was believed that Langevin was "unhappily married to a woman who came from a similar working-class background but lacked his educational attainments."[2] Langevin felt his wife did not have an appreciation of his work or his contributions as a scientist. He found that Marie Curie did, so it was understandable to many that the two would develop a close relationship. Unfortunately, Curie's fame and Langevin's standing in the scientific community left them both with little privacy.

It was while Curie was en route to a scientific conference in Brussels at the end of October, 1911, that news broke of a rumored affair between her and Langevin. Renowned Belgian manufacturer and philanthropist Ernest Solvay had extended invitations for an all-expenses-paid trip to Brussels to several top European and English physicists for an international conference. Solvay's ambitious convention sparked a lot of interest and was seen as "possibly the greatest gathering of scientific brainpower ever concentrated in one room at the same time."[3] During the historic conference (the first of many Solvay congresses held over the years), the distinguished group had the opportunity to gather to discuss and learn about each other's work. Among those invited were Max Planck, Ernest Rutherford, Albert Einstein, Paul Langevin, and Marie Curie.

The story of the affair between Curie and Langevin first gained life in the Paris paper *Le Journal*, where Curie was described as a "husband-snatcher." *Le Journal* founder Fernand Xau had "plastered a two-column article entitled 'A History of Love: Mme. Curie and Professor Langevin.'"[4] Included in the article was an interview that had taken place between journalist F. Hauser and Mme. Langevin's mother, Mme. Desfosses. Desfosses claimed to have knowledge of letters written between Curie and her son-in-law that provided proof of the alleged affair. Curie attempted to put the rumored affair to rest in a handwritten note she gave to a correspondent of the Paris paper *Le Temps*. In the note Curie "stated categorically that she attached no importance to rumors based on 'pure fantasy.'"[5] Nonetheless, the story took center stage in several papers and soon became the buzz of conversation and eyebrow-raising in and around the conference.

At the end of the Solvay conference, Langevin and

Curie disappeared—separately. When yet another paper, *L'Intransigent*, published its own Langevin-Curie affair story, an already ill and upset Curie wrote a stronger letter. "I consider the intrusions of the press and public into my private life abominable. . . . I will undertake vigorous action against the publication of writings attributed to me."[6] Shortly after Curie's letter appeared in *Le Temps*, she received an apology from *Le Journal* writer F. Hauser. It was unfortunate that the story of the rumored affair died out slowly, almost superceding more important and profoundly impressive news that Curie had been selected by the Royal Swedish Academy of Sciences to receive the coveted Nobel Prize in Chemistry for her continued work with the elements radium and polonium.

The 1911 Nobel Prize was Curie's second. Her first was shared in 1903 with husband Pierre and Henri Becquerel for their joint discovery of radioactivity. On its own merits, the Nobel still ranks as one of the world's most prestigious awards. To date, only Marie Curie, American physicist John Bardeen (1965, 1972), and British biochemist Frederick Sanger (1958, 1980) have been the recipients of two Nobel prizes in fields of science. This marks Curie's accomplishment as one of the greatest not only for scientists, but for all women who conduct their research and work in a largely male-dominated field.

Despite a continued state of frail health, Marie Curie made the forty-eight-hour trip from Sceaux, France, to Stockholm, Sweden, in December to collect her award in person. Accompanied on the trip by her sister Bronya and daughter Irène, Curie stood in the great Hall of Prizes in the Stockholm Royal Palace on December 10, 1911, to

MARIE CURIE IS ONE OF THE MOST IMPORTANT FIGURES IN THE HISTORY OF SCIENCE.

receive her Nobel medal and leather-bound certificate from King Gustav V. The citation on the award given to Curie read: "In recognition of her services to the advancement of chemistry by the discovery of the elements radium and polonium, by the isolation of radium and the study of the nature and compounds of this remarkable element."[7]

As is customary for each Nobel laureate, on the following day Curie delivered a lecture entitled "Radium and the New Concepts in Chemistry," during which she discussed the importance of her work with radium. A humble Curie first acknowledged the earlier contributions of the men who helped forge the way for her own work to continue. She began by honoring Henri Becquerel for his discovery of radiation in uranium, then moved on to discuss the expansion of radiation research into other substances by her husband Pierre and herself:

> All the elements emitting such radiation I have termed *radioactive*, and the new property of matter revealed in this emission has thus received the name *radioactivity*. Thanks to this discovery of new, very powerful radioactive substances, particularly radium, the study of radioactivity progressed with marvellous [sic] rapidity: Discoveries followed each other in rapid succession, and it was obvious that a new science was in course of development.[8]

Curie did not fail to mention the continuation of scientific devotion to the study of radioactivity, most notably by 1908 Nobel laureate Ernest Rutherford. Emphasizing the importance of the research, Curie went on to say, "in this field the importance of radium from the viewpoint of general theories has been decisive. The history of the discovery and the isolation of this substance has furnished proof of my hypothesis that radioactivity is an atomic property of matter and can provide a means of seeking new elements."[9]

In concluding her opening remarks before beginning the specifics of her lecture on successes in isolating radium, Curie said:

> Viewing the subject from this angle, it can be said that the task of isolating radium is the cornerstone of the edifice of the science of radioactivity. Moreover, radium remains the most useful and powerful tool in radioactivity laboratories. I believe that it is because of these considerations that the Swedish Academy of Sciences has done me the very great honour of awarding me this year's Nobel Prize for Chemistry.[10]

In true character, Curie did not forget to pay homage to her dear husband, Pierre, reminding her colleagues that the work for which she was receiving this award was intimately connected with their common work, which the Academy of Sciences had acknowledged in awarding the Nobel Prize in Physics to Pierre, Marie, and Henri Becquerel in 1903. In Curie's mind, by honoring her, the Nobel Academy was honoring the memory of Pierre Curie as well. No matter what people believed, no matter what the tabloids reported, her devotion to Pierre's memory would always be maintained.

CHAPTER TWO

OPPRESSION AND TRAGEDY IN POLAND

The nineteenth-century world in which Marie Salomée Sklodowska was born did not favor her Polish heritage. For almost one hundred years her nation had been subjected to the harsh, oppressive rule of its Russian neighbors, the latest in a long line of countries that had partitioned Poland's lands as part of the spoils of war. Several failed uprisings by the Poles against their oppressors in 1831 and again in 1863 resulted in severe retaliation and restrictive governance. Captured insurgents were either hanged or exiled to hard labor in the frozen tundra of Siberia. In their place came the watchdogs of the oppressor—police, teachers, and local officials—who were brought in to wear down any symbols of Polish nationalism. At the time of Marie's birth, what had once been Poland was currently ruled by His Majesty Alexander II, Czar of All the Russias. Under his reign, almost every aspect of Polish life—its history, culture, language, and customs—were blotted out in favor of everything Russian.

Born near the ancient city of Warsaw on November 7, 1867, Marie (affectionately called Manya by her parents) was the fifth and last child of Władysłav and Bronisława Skłodowski. (The spelling of Polish surnames may vary according to gender and marital status.) Both parents were zealous patriots, and though not themselves activists, had not been left untouched by the unrest in their homeland. Władyslav and Bronisława had married in the summer of 1860, as the latest Polish unrest was gaining strength toward another rebellion. In what became known as the January Uprising of 1863 (a revolt against the Russian occupation of Poland), Władysłav's brother, Zdzisław, had been wounded twice. Later, he would flee to France, along with one hundred thousand other Poles, to avoid punishment. Bronisława's brother, Henryk, also joined the battle, only to be captured and exiled to Siberia.

By the time the January Uprising was defeated, the Skłodowskis were living on Freta Street in apartments adjacent to the school where Bronisława worked as headmistress. As with most things, being in such a position had its advantages and disadvantages. After the 1863 uprising, the Poles decided to shift tactics. Instead of fighting on the battlefield, they would educate and train the young minds coming up in their society. Outwardly the new "patriots" would appear to conform to their Russification, but they would gain the very occupations—schoolteachers, artists, intellectuals, religious leaders—that would allow them to influence the youth of their county's future.

RUSSIAN

KINGDOM OF
NORWAY
AND SWEDEN

DEN-
MARK

BALTIC
SEA

EMPIRE

BRITISH
ISLES

• Warsaw

NETHER-
LANDS

P R U S S I A

BEL-
GIUM

GERMAN
STATES

• Paris

AUSTRIA-

FRANCE

HUNGARY

MOLDAVIA

SWITZ.

BLACK
SEA

ITALY

O T T O M A N   E M P I R E

SPAIN

MEDITERRANEAN   SEA

GREECE

c. 1867

THE BOUNDARIES OF EUROPEAN NATIONS AS THEY EXISTED AT THE TIME
OF MARIE CURIE'S BIRTH IN 1867.

The Skłodowskis set good examples for their children, Zosia (1862), Józef (1863), Bronisława (1865), Helena (1866), and Maria (1867). Władysłav and Bronisława both came from an unusual Polish form of land nobility known as *szlachta*. However, nobility did not necessarily equate with wealth. By the time the Skłodowski and Boguski families greeted the nineteenth century, their noble heritages did nothing to improve their economic positions in Polish society. The Skłodowskis overcame those economic and cultural adversities, however, later forming a good marriage and a solid family foundation for their children. Years later their son, Józef, would say, "My father was concerned about our health, our physical development, our studies and even our free time, for which he tried to provide us with ideas and games."[1]

Bronisława was the eldest daughter of Felix Boguski and Maria Zaruska. The Boguskis were too poor to live on their own estate, but they were able enough to oversee the property of wealthier families. Still, Bronisława and her sisters attended the Freta Street school, the only private girls' school in Warsaw. Though opportunities for women were much less available than those for their male counterparts, Bronisława received an excellent education, became a gifted pianist, and eventually rose from student to teacher and finally headmistress of the school. She was twenty-four years old when she married Władysłav Skłodowski, a man four years older than she was.

Władysłav, too, came from an educated, middle-class family. His father, Josef, once a soldier in the 1830 uprising, eventually left the country life to teach physics and mathematics at an all boys' gymnasium (high school) in Lublin.

MARIE IS PICTURED HERE WITH HER FATHER, WŁADYSŁAV, AND HER SISTERS, BRONYA AND HELA.

Władysław followed in his father's footsteps, applying himself to his studies. After taking his advanced educational training at the University of St. Petersburg, Władysław returned to Warsaw to teach mathematics and physics. He fell in love with the beautiful Freta Street schoolteacher Bronisława Boguska, and when the two wed in 1860, theirs was viewed as a very suitable marriage.

Because of Mme. Skłodowski's position as headmistress of Freta Street, the family was able to live in an apartment on the first floor of the school. They lived there for eight years before Władysław, recognizing that he needed to supplement the family's income, left the school where he was teaching to take a post as professor and under-inspector at a boys' gymnasium. The gymnasium was on Novolipki Street at the western end of Warsaw near the Jewish Quarter. The Skłodowskis would live in various apartments in and around this neighborhood for the next twenty years. Moving to Novolipki Street made it too difficult for Mme. Skłodowski to continue as principal of the girls' school. Aside from the distance, she was now in frail health and trying to raise a family that had grown to five children. With regret, Mme. Skłodowski, who just six months before had given birth to her last child, little Manya, gave up her post at Freta Street.

It was not a good time to be a Pole and belong to the vibrant, educated class in a society that stifled anything that appeared Polish, especially if you were an educator. As Eve Curie noted in her book *Madame Curie*: "Beneath the affectations of politeness a profound antagonism existed between conqueror and conquered throughout the Polish schools—between the harassed teachers and the spying principals."[2] For Professor Skłodowski, "the spying principal" was M. Ivanov, director of the gymnasium and therefore a representative of the government of the Czar. An ignorant, detestable man, Ivanov relentlessly scoured the students' written work looking for any signs of forbidden "Polishisms." At best, Skłodowski and Ivanov had a curt working relationship.

Even as a young schoolchild, Manya was subjected to rigid Russification in class. Her teacher, Mlle. Antonia Tupalska, secretly held Polish history lessons that could be stopped at a moment's notice. A bell would ring to warn of Russian inspectors coming to the school. One day, inspector Vysokorodye Hornberg came to Manya's class and called on the frightened young girl. He fired off several questions to Manya: "Name the Tsars who have reigned over our Holy Russia since Catherine II . . . who rules over us?"[3] Manya hesitated to answer until Hornberg asked her again for the third time, an anger in his voice that told her to comply. She answered, "His Majesty Alexander II, Tsar of All the Russias."[4] Satisfied, Hornberg turned on his heels and left, at which point Manya dissolved in tears.

Once home, Manya could brush off the fear and anger she felt in class. She longed for comfort from her mother, but it was a rarity to receive anything more than a pat on the head or a quick hug from Mme. Skłodowski. Manya did not really understand why her mother withheld affection, but it was really for her own safety. Sometime after Marie was born, Mme. Skłodowski developed tuberculosis, an infectious disease that attacks the respiratory system and was often fatal. To protect her family, Mme. Skłodowski ate off dishes she reserved for her own use and limited her physical contact with the family to hugs but no kissing. Still, as a family, the Skłodowskis spent many hours together. Mme. Skłodowski had taught herself to make shoes and mend the children's clothing, since it was difficult to leave the house. On Saturday evenings she would join her children in the living room while her husband read aloud from the many literary classics adorning his bookcase. It was Professor Skłodow Skłodowski's way of incorporating family time with educating his children.

As Manya grew older, the cruelties and unpleasantness of the world became much more vivid. Mme. Skłodowski's condition had not improved, and Władysłav finally scraped together enough money to send his wife and daughter Zosia to Nice, France, so that his wife might get well. Manya was without the companionship of her beloved mother for a year. When Mme. Skłodowski and Zosia returned, Manya saw an even weaker, frailer-looking woman than the one who'd left the year before. Things had not been going well between Professor Skłodowski and M. Ivanov, either. After returning from a vacation with relatives in the country, Władysłav found a letter waiting for him from his employer. It informed him that his salary was being reduced, he was being stripped of his under-inspector title, and the family's lodgings were being taken away. This devastating news would begin a period of decline for the Skłodowskis, and they found themselves moving several times before settling in a small corner apartment at Novolipki and Carmelite streets in western Warsaw.

As Władysłav's fortunes continued to slide, he was forced to take in boarders and offer private instruction to supplement the family's dwindling income. At first it was just two or three boarders, then five, eight, and even ten at a time. The crowded apartment forced the Skłodowski children to adjust to strangers living in their midst. Young Manya slept on an animal skin on the sofa in the dining room. She had to rise at 6:00 A.M. so that the table could be set for breakfast. Studying might have been a challenge with so many people bustling about, but Manya had an intense concentration well beyond her years. She was able to tune out all distractions once she settled in with her books.

Unfortunately, in January 1874, the boarders brought more to the home than their money. A few of them brought typhus (a disease that causes bleeding and skin rashes) into the house. Not long after, both Zosia and Bronya contracted the disease. Bronya recovered; Zosia eventually died. Years later all of the surviving children concurred that Zosia's death was a blow from which their own frail mother could never recover. Holding her father's hand tightly, nine-year-old Manya walked with Józef and Helena behind Zosia's coffin as they headed toward Powazki cemetery to bury their sister. Bronya, still too sick, and Mme. Skłodowski, too weak, could only watch the funeral procession as it passed by the apartment window.

Bronisława Skłodowski lived for another two years after Zosia's death. The Skłodowski family even managed to take another vacation in the country, relaxing at Gdynska Colony, near Gdansk. Władysłav wrote to Józef, who was vacationing elsewhere, of the pleasantness that surrounded them: "[B]irds twitter and sing all the time; besides that—silence and the strong, nice smell of resin in the air. After the dust and noise of Warsaw, this is simply delightful."[5]

The news was not all light, however, as Władysłav also commented that he wished Mme. Skłodowski's health had shown some improvement.

On May 9, 1878, Bronisława Skłodowski passed away at home in the family apartment in Warsaw. The day before she had summoned the children into her room, made the sign of the cross above each of their heads, and told them that she loved them all. For the second time in two years, a still young Manya walked in a funeral procession to bury another member of the family. At age eleven, Marie had suddenly found herself without her eldest sister's companionship and guidance, and without the tenderness and love of her mother. She found it difficult to invoke the same love of God that she had before Zosia and Mme. Skłodowski died.

Despite the tragedy absorbed by the Skłodowski children, all four grew to overcome adversity and become successful in their own right. Bronya finished her studies in grand fashion, winning a gold medal at the government gymnasium. In the same school, Manya was one of the most brilliant pupils in attendance. Bronya headed the household, keeping the books and tracking the comings and goings of countless boarders. Józef too had finished his studies at the boys' school with a gold medal, and he was studying at the Faculty of Medicine.

Life for Manya after her mother's death continued to be a blurred combination of school and home. She had been known as the child of a teacher, she had lived in the family quarters of a school, and her own teacher, Antonia Tupalska, had moved in with the Skłodowskis when Mme. Skłodowski's health worsened. It seemed that the word *gymnasium* was a regular part of her world, and in some ways, as Eve Curie wrote in *Madame Curie*, "Manya must have grown to imagine the universe as an immense school where there were only teachers and pupils and where only one ideal reigned: to learn."[6]

The pressure from learning on a "double schedule"—Russian studies for the authorities, and clandestine studies of Polish language, history, and geography—must have been enormous on Manya and her classmates. Constantly on alert for a surprise visit and having to switch gears so quickly created an environment of anxiety, fear, and great expectations. And Manya was a year younger than her classmates. Still, she seemed to do well. She was bright, articulate, and had a tremendous power of concentration cultivated over years out of necessity.

> *"I feel everything very violently, with a physical violence."*
>
> **—Marie Curie**

Since the other Skłodowski children were bright and obtaining good grades, it was assumed that Manya was also. But she was hiding a deep pain within. The only indication that something was amiss was Manya's "strong and quickly aroused emotions." When Curie was older and able to reflect on her early years, she wrote, "I feel everything very violently, with a physical violence."[7] The reaction may have been from an accumulation of anxiety—since age five she had watched her mother's health deteriorate; she felt abandoned during her mother's long absences; she lost her beloved Zosia to illness; and finally her greatest fear came to fruition when her mother succumbed to her own battle with tuberculosis.

There may have been early signs that Marie was battling with depression. She was just fifteen years old when she finished her studies at the gymnasium. On June 12, 1883, the third gold medal for scholastic excellence was handed out to one of Władysłav Skłodowski's children. This one went to his little Manya. After the ceremony, Manya said her farewells and headed home with a father bursting with pride. If he was concerned about his daughter's mental health, he did not say so. She was still too young to consider marriage, and had herself expressed feeling exhausted. Władysłav decided that Manya should set aside any further intellectual interests for the moment and take a year to recuperate from the long ordeals of her youth. Shortly after graduation, an ecstatic Marie boarded a train and headed off to stay with her uncles Henryk and Władysłav Boguski in the beautiful countryside of Mazovia. For the next year, Marie would rest, dance, relax, and laugh, enjoying freedom from any of the rigidity or pressures that had been in her life.

CHAPTER THREE

THE LONG ROAD TO PARIS

The year Marie Curie spent away from her home in Warsaw was one of the happiest times in her life. She wrote to her friend Kazia:

> I have no schedule, I get up sometimes at ten o'clock, sometimes at four or five (morning, not evening!). I read no serious books, only harmless and absurd little novels. . . . Thus, in spite of the diploma conferring on me the dignity and maturity of a person who has finished her studies, I feel incredibly stupid. Sometimes I laugh all by myself, and I contemplate my state of total stupidity with genuine satisfaction.[1]

Marie spent the year traveling among her various uncles, aunts, and cousins, completely free of all of life's pressures. She developed a passion for the country, enjoying seeing the change of seasons, learning how to ride horseback, and enchanted by the snowy, sparkling peaks of the Carpathians. She spent joyous hours walking along footpaths lined with bilberries, marveling at the craftsmanship of the mountaineers' cottages set all along the way.

Time spent with her uncle Zdzisław in Galicia was always full of surprises. The house was always filled with laughter, as Zdzisłav, his wife, and three daughters seemed to soak in the joy of everyday life like it was a constant celebration. Guests came and went, so the house was always full of commotion for planning large festive dinners, baking, and adorning costumes for the next *kulig*. "The *kulig*, or sleigh party, was a centuries-old Polish tradition in which horse-drawn sleighs of revelers, with torches flaring and sleigh bells jangling, travel from one manor house to the next."[2]

Disguised as Cracow peasants, Marie and her cousins took off in their sleigh, escorted by men on horseback lighting the way with their torches. Music filled the air as the sleighs met up with others on their way to someone's house, the first to play host to the evening's festivities. After a quick meal with musical accompaniment, everything was packed up and the sleighs would be on their way to the next house. The *kulig* went on for two days and became one of Marie's favorite memories of her time away from home.

The ending of Marie's idyllic year was prolonged through the summer, thanks to an old student of their mother. Marie and her sister Helena were to be guests at Kepa, the luxurious country estate of Count Ludwik de Fleury and his much younger wife, Bronisława's former pupil. Marie again wrote Kazia:

I ought to give you an account of our existence here—
but as I haven't the courage, I shall only say that it is
marvelous . . . there is plenty of water for swimming and
boating, which delights me. I am learning to row—I am
getting on quite well—and the bathing is ideal. We do
everything that comes into our heads, we sleep sometimes at night and sometimes by day, we dance, and we
run to such follies that sometimes we deserve to be
locked up in an asylum for the insane.[3]

The year 1884 was a whirlwind time for sixteen-year-
old Marie. It was to be the only truly carefree time she
would ever know in her sixty-seven-year life. The memories,
however, always remained. Years later Helena wrote, "The
summer passed as quickly as a dream, but the memory of it
has been lasting. How many times did Manya and I talk
about [it] . . . and every time we would smile, and even
shed a tear of nostalgia. It is good when a person has had
at least one such crazy summer in her life."[4]

Marie and Helena returned to the apartment on
Novolipki Street at summer's end. For the first time in
many years Władysłav decided not to take in any more
boarders, so the family had to move to smaller quarters
nearby. Money was tight—Władysłav's savings had been
depleted, he was just a few years away from retirement, and
Józef was still at Warsaw University, pursuing a degree in
medicine. The only advanced schooling opportunities for
women were in Geneva, Switzerland, and Paris, France.
Bronya was determined to go abroad to medical school, but
she needed to earn enough money to do so. After a brief
discussion between the two sisters, they decided to place
ads offering tutoring services.

Tutoring proved to be a very ungratifying job.

Sometimes students showed, sometimes they did not. Those that did show were often late. Many times an absent-minded student would forget to pay what he owed at the end of the month. Marie accepted her circumstances, vowing that they were only temporary. Meanwhile she continued to seek ways to sustain her own educational growth. She became involved with the other intellectuals in and around Warsaw who looked to embrace new ideas that were seeping in from the West. She read the philosophical writings of Auguste Comte, who was the founder of positivism. Comte believed that much of philosophy and theology up to that point were based too much on theory, when in fact there were many positive, observable phenomena that could provide answers to life's basic questions. He also wrote and lectured on limiting the powers of the church in government, and on allowing everyone, including women, to receive a quality education.[5]

Because education was not yet available to everyone in Poland, Marie began her advanced-level education through an acquaintance, Mlle. Piasecka. Piasecka was running an illegal night school dubbed the Floating University. Admission was free, so Bronya joined too. "Because it appealed simultaneously to her patriotism, her intellectual aspirations, and her humanitarianism, Manya was soon one of the Floating University's most enthusiastic members."[6]

Participating was risky, however. Since it was a Polish school operating beyond the watchful eye of the Russian inspector, those taking part could be subject to criminal prosecution, prison, or even exile to Siberia if they were discovered. Classes were held secretly in abandoned buildings, cellars, or friends' homes, with no more than a dozen gathered in one place. Mlle. Piasecka's hope was that by creating the Floating University, she could help contribute to the development of the country's intellectuals, who would then in turn continue the education of others, perhaps working toward liberating Poland.

This time was very critical in Marie's personal and professional development. Unable to find solace in the church and her religion after the deaths of her mother and sister, Marie gravitated toward positivism and quantifiable reason. Meanwhile she gladly offered to give lessons to poor women, immediately beginning to pass the torch of knowledge by reading to workers in a dressmaking factory. As Eve Curie writes about her mother during that period: "She dreamed no longer of mathematics or chemistry alone, but wished to reform the established order and enlighten the masses of the people."[7]

Soon, the realities of the Skłodowska family's financial needs pulled Marie away from her own pursuits. Even though Bronya had managed to save enough money to go to Paris and cover expenses for the first year of medical school, Marie realized it would take several years before enough money was saved to cover the five-year course. Together the sisters decided that Bronya would go to Paris to begin her studies while Marie took a job as a live-in governess. Marie would send Bronya the majority of her earnings so that Bronya could complete school. When she earned her degree, Bronya would send for Marie and subsidize Marie's education.

Soon after the pact was made between the sisters, a grateful Bronya headed off to Paris to study at the Sorbonne. Marie's first governess job was a disaster and lasted only about six weeks. However, not long after her return to Warsaw, she was offered a three-year contract with a salary of 500 rubles a year to work for the Zorawski family in the sugar beet region of Szczuki. Though the job was an excellent opportunity, the day of her departure from Warsaw was one of the dreariest in her life. A three-hour rail ride and a four-hour sleigh ride lay ahead of her on a cold, snowy January day, 1886.

Marie settled into an uneventful routine with her new family. Two of the Zorawski children, Bronka, one year her junior, and ten-year-old Andzia, would receive their schooling from Marie. Conversation at the dinner table consisted mainly of discussion about running the sugar beet factory, and local gossip. One day when Marie discovered the deplorable conditions under which the peasants who worked the fields were living, she began to give them two hours of schooling on her own time.

When summer arrived, Marie decided not to take any time off, even though she was fairly homesick. She had often corresponded with her father, brother, and cousin Henrietta by letter. In many of her letters Marie sounded rather resigned and depressed, wondering if she would ever take that train ride to Paris and study at the Sorbonne like Bronya. At the very least, Marie sounded lonely. In one such letter to her cousin, however, for the first time Marie refers to romance. "Some people pretend . . . I am obliged to pass through the kind of fever called love." She goes on to write, "This absolutely does not enter into my plans. If I ever had any others, they have gone up in smoke; I have buried them; locked them up; sealed and forgotten them."[8]

Though Marie never made specific reference to a love affair, it seems that there had been one.

Casimir, the eldest son of the Zorawskis, had come home from Warsaw over the holidays. When he arrived, he found a young, pretty governess in the house, "who could dance marvelously, row and skate; who was witty and had nice manners; who could make up verses as easily as she rode a horse or drove a carriage; who was different—how totally, mysteriously different!—from all the young ladies of his acquaintance."[9] In time Casimir and Marie fell in love, but it was not to last. When Casimir informed his parents of his intention to marry Marie, they flew into a rage. No son of theirs was going to marry beneath him, least of all to a penniless woman who worked in other people's homes to make a living. As it turned out, Marie's young love had not the backbone to defy his parents, and the relationship ended.

As hurt as she was, Marie was also coldly practical. Despite the outright rejection from the Zorawskis, she stayed and continued in her role as governess and teacher. To pass the remaining two years on her contract, Marie stepped up her correspondence to her family, offering them advice, encouragement, and to Bronya, her money. She also continued self-study, borrowing books from the factory library, and drifted increasingly toward an interest in the sciences.

Release came for Marie during the Easter holiday, 1889. After three long years she returned home. Wladyslav had retired, was collecting an adequate pension, and had taken a job as director of a reformatory at Studziwniec. He also began to send Bronya money, and soon she was able to tell

Marie to stop sending her own money. Marie took on one more governess assignment, a one-year contract with a well-to-do family in Sopot, an upscale beach area in the Baltic region. Life resumed rather uneventfully until Marie received a letter from Bronya informing her that she was planning to marry a medical student, Kazimierz Dłuski. They planned to spend one more year in Paris before returning home, so Bronya invited Marie to come to Paris the following year and live with them while she began her studies at the Sorbonne. Marie declined over her sister's objections, preferring to have one more year to save money before departing for Paris.

When at last her work obligation in Sopot was completed, Marie returned home and settled back into life with her father in Warsaw. She resumed her attendance at the Floating University, and for the first time in her life stepped into a laboratory. Her cousin, Joseph Boguski, was the director of what was called the Museum of Industry and Agriculture. The unassuming building at 66 Krakovsky Boulevard was just a front for what went on beyond its doors. Though her time there was limited, and she often found herself working alone, it was there that she conducted her first chemistry experiments. Of the experience, Marie wrote, "I developed my taste for experimental research during these first trials."[10] After years of uncertainty about a vocation, Marie's career plans suddenly came into focus.

Almost eight years had passed since Marie graduated from the gymnasium. As much as she felt torn leaving her father and beloved Poland, shortly before her twenty-fourth birthday Marie boarded the transcontinental train that would take her to Paris. She traveled light—most of her things had been packed earlier and shipped ahead to Bronya. Excited about her new journey, Marie finally allowed herself to think about her future. Going to Paris let two traits blossom that Marie would carry for the rest of her life—unabated ambition and independence.

The trip to Paris was long and grueling, a three-day, thousand-mile journey, but Marie was too overwhelmed by being in Paris to care. Her new brother-in-law, Kazimierz, met her at the train station, and before long they were at their home, a second-floor apartment at Rue d'Allemagne. Though it was wonderful to see her sister again, now several months pregnant, Marie sometimes felt distracted by the constant flow of guests being entertained in the Dluski home. Early for the fall semester, Marie decided to use some of her time to explore the wonders of Paris. In her native Warsaw, Marie had only read about the historic city; now she traveled past the Seine River, the cathedral of Notre Dame, and of course the Sorbonne. As she stood there looking at the building, Marie almost couldn't believe she was really and truly in France and about to begin her advanced educational training.

At registration, Marie signed in as Mlle. Marie Skłodowska. After an initial difficulty adjusting to the French style of education, Marie soon fell right in step. "The student who comes to France," she observed, "should not expect to find direction towards a utilitarian goal right at the start. The French system consists essentially of awakening the student's confidence in his own abilities and fostering the habit of using them."[11] Not long after she enjoyed the freedom at the Sorbonne, Marie also experienced the freedom of living on her own. Leaving behind the constant distractions at her sister's, Marie moved into a small, single-room apartment in a sixth-floor attic in the Latin Quarter, an artists' and students' community near the Sorbonne.

The advantage of being on the top floor was gazing out at the glittering view of Paris. The disadvantage, besides the long climb up the stairs, was that it was extremely cold and drafty. Many nights to keep warm, Marie piled all of her clothing on top of the bedcovers. She had a small stove on which she cooked meager meals—a piece of "bread with a cup of chocolate, eggs or fruit." Still, Marie "looked back on this 'period of solitary years exclusively devoted to the studies . . . for which I had waited so long' as 'one of the best memories of my life.'"[12]

It was a great time to be studying at the Sorbonne. A group of faculty members were onboard, ones who were able to inspire their students instead of just rote teaching. Marie's teachers included Gabriel Lippmann, who would win the 1908 Nobel Prize in Physics; Paul Painlevé, a mathematician who would hold many high offices in government, including French minister of war; and Henri Poincaré, a preeminent mathematician and writer of the late nineteenth century who made important contributions to mathematical theory. Marie wrote, "In the life of the laboratories, the influence of the professors on the students is due to their own love of science and to their personal qualities much more than to their authority."[13] She allowed little time for anything other than her studies in her three years at the Sorbonne.

Marie's academic success was remarkable. She passed

the exam for her *licence ès sciences* (the equivalent of a master's degree), ranking first among those who sat for the exam. One degree was originally all Marie had planned to earn. She had wanted to return to Warsaw to teach, but when her friend Jadwiga Dydyńska managed to secure a 600-ruble scholarship for her, Marie happily decided to pursue a second degree, this time in mathematics. Again, Marie was scholastically triumphant. Earning her *licence ès mathématiques* in July 1894, the girl who had had such difficulty in math at the Warsaw gymnasium finished second in the exam.

The following spring Marie was commissioned by the Society for the Encouragement of National Industry to research the relationship between magnetic properties of various steels and their chemical composition. She began her work in the laboratory of Professor Lippmann, but soon found that she needed more space for the equipment necessary for testing and analyzing her experiments. A chance meeting with a friend from her days as governess in Szczuki would provide the perfect solution. Professor Kowalski, husband of the friend, taught physics at the University of Fribourg in Switzerland. He had given some lectures in Paris and had made the acquaintance of a prominent scientist who worked at the School of Physics and Chemistry on Rue Lhomond. Kowalski thought perhaps the scientist could offer some solution to Marie's problem. He invited Marie to his hotel the next day so that he could introduce her to Pierre Curie.

CHAPTER FOUR

RESEARCH LEADS TO DISCOVERY

For the rest of her life, Marie would clearly remember her first glimpse of Pierre Curie. "He seemed to me very young," she recalled years later, "though he was at that time thirty-five years old. I was struck by the open expression of his face and by the slight suggestion of detachment in his whole attitude. His speech, rather slow and deliberate, his simplicity, and his smile, at once grave and youthful, inspired confidence."[1]

Pierre was working at a new and lesser-known institution than the Society for the Encouragement of National Industry, and he was less celebrated than perhaps he should have been. The main reason was that he worked outside the traditional scientific circles of his time. He had studied at home rather than attend one of the better French academies. When Marie met him, he had not received his Ph.D.

but he had done the work required for the degree several times over. He was teaching at a new, unknown school—the École Municipale de Physique et Chimie Industrielle (EPCI), also known as the School of Physics and Chemistry—instead of at a prestigious school such as the Sorbonne. When singled out to receive specific scientific honors for his achievements, he invariably turned them down. "I have decided never to accept any decoration of any sort," he wrote to the founder and director of the EPCI in response to a proposal that he be awarded an honorary title. "If you obtain this honor for me, you will obligate me to refuse it."[2] Pierre Curie's deepest desire was to be left alone to continue his research privately, without fanfare.

Pierre's father, Eugène Curie, and grandfather, Paul Curie, were both men of principle whose strong convictions were not always accepted by society. Pierre was born in Paris on May 15, 1859, the second son of Sophie-Claire Depouilly and Eugène Curie. Sophie-Claire's father was a prominent businessman from a town on the outskirts of Paris; both he and Sophie-Claire's brothers were industrial inventors. Eugène, on the other hand, was a physician, as was his father, Paul.

Paul Curie was a respected doctor in Mulhouse, in the Alsace region of France. But in 1831, he announced publicly that he had come to believe in Saint-Simonianism. This movement's followers included many of French society's most highly regarded intellectuals. They believed that they had developed a "new society" in which each person would work and live according to his or her true calling. In Saint-Simonianism, women were spiritually important and war and aggression had no place, nor did hierarchy based on wealth and status.

Dr. Curie's new beliefs were not greeted warmly by the townspeople of Mulhouse. He was demoted from his high position in the Protestant church, and his life in town became so difficult that he moved to England. His wife stayed in Paris with the children. For this reason, Eugène, the oldest of the four, never really knew his father. However, he grew to believe in similar principles and chose his father's profession. After medical school, he studied anatomy at Paris's Museum of Natural History, but for lack of money he had to leave academia and become a practicing physician. In 1848, during a political revolution in France, he joined the rebels manning the barricades of the capital city, and during the reign that followed, Eugène, because he had been wounded, became a decorated warrior.

Eugène's unpopular political affiliations made it difficult for him to attract patients from Paris high society, and he was forced to work for low pay as school physician for the government. Although the family was affected financially—Pierre and his older brother, Jacques, were forced to make difficult choices of their own—the Curie children learned a great deal from their father. Throughout their younger years, they took long jaunts with Eugène into the countryside, where he taught them about plant and animal life. The three also enjoyed long afternoons of swimming and hiking. Pierre would remember those days as some of the finest of his life.

Eugène educated his children at home, but soon realized that Pierre in particular would need more professional guidance. Marie Curie would later write that Pierre needed

PIERRE AND MARIE CURIE, CIRCA 1895.

"to concentrate his thought with great intensity upon a certain definite object, in order to obtain a precise result."[3] His focus was so intense that other aspects of his schooling, such as the study of literature and the classics, fell by the wayside. Eugène hired a tutor, Albert Bazille, for Pierre, and it paid off. At sixteen, Pierre earned a bachelor of science degree and entered the Sorbonne. Two years later, he received the Sorbonne's *licence ès sciences* and became an assistant in the school's physics lab. Before long, Pierre had published the results of his research, first with Paul Desains, one of his professors, and then with his brother, Jacques.

Jacques and Pierre's first official collaboration was on the study of crystals. The brothers wanted to discover what lay behind the curious symmetry of crystal formation. In 1880, they announced their finding that pressure, not heat, caused crystal substances to give off an electric charge. This discovery of "polar electricity" was published in the *Bulletin of the Mineralogy Society*. They also invented an instrument, the piezoelectric quartz balance, that could measure extremely small amounts of electrical charge, as well as several other scientific devices.

In 1883 Jacques received a professorship in mineralogy at the University of Montpellier, while Pierre was named chief of laboratories at EPCI in Paris. He continued pursuing his work on crystals when he was not teaching laboratory students. Most people who knew Pierre considered this an unworthy position for him, however. "From the scientific point of view, it is certain that his appointment to this school . . . slowed by several years his experimental research," Jacques later said. "These were hard years of assiduous work, which were useful mainly to the students he formed and educated."[4]

While at EPCI, Pierre Curie invented and constructed a supersensitive scientific scale called the Curie scale, discovered a basic law of magnetism that became known as Curie's law, and formed the principle of symmetry that is one of the foundations of modern science. And yet "[f]or these efforts, crowned by dazzling success, and for the constant care he lavished on the thirty students confided to him," wrote his daughter Eve Curie in 1937, "[he] was receiving from the French State, in 1894 . . . a salary of three hundred francs a month—just about what a specialized worker would receive in a factory."[5]

The following summer, Jacques returned from Montpellier and joined Pierre to continue their combined research. Jacques had married, and Pierre, who had been disappointed in love earlier in life, was nearly resigned to being a life-long bachelor. When he met Marie Sklodowski, however, Pierre found himself smitten with the young woman.

After their first meeting in his lab, Pierre met Marie several more times at the sessions of the Physics Society, during which scientists would present reports on new research. He sent her a copy of his publication, *On Symmetry in Physical Phenomena: Symmetry of an Electric Field and of a Magnetic Field*, inscribing it "To Mlle Sklodowska, with the respect and friendship of the author, P. Curie."[6] Finally, he asked Marie if he could pay her a call at home. He found that she lived in a tiny attic room that was almost bare of furnishings. Far from seeming less attractive in her poor surroundings,

Marie, standing in the room in an old, worn dress, seemed to Pierre more beautiful than ever.

Marie and Pierre had the same strong familial ties, the same love of science and culture, and the same levels of affection between parents and children. Their own relationship was also one of scientific accord. As they grew to know one another better, Marie convinced Pierre to begin work on a doctoral thesis, and to make his experiments on magnetism the subject. In March 1895, about a year after they met, Marie attended Pierre's defense of his doctoral thesis at the Sorbonne.

Armed with his Ph.D., Pierre received a professorship at the School of Physics and Chemistry. Not long after, he and Jacques were awarded (and they accepted) the Prix Planté for their work on piezoelectricity. But Pierre's life took an even more joyful turn when Marie decided to join him in France, having overcome her reservations about settling away from Poland. They were married in a small, quiet ceremony on July 26, 1895, in the town hall at Sceaux.

In addition to juggling household and professional responsibilities, Marie was also taking on another task: she aimed to earn a certificate allowing her to educate young women in the physical sciences. She continued to research the magnetic properties of steel and convinced the director of EPCI to permit her to complete her work on school grounds—although she received no financial support from the school.

When in 1897 Marie submitted her research results to the Society for the Encouragement of National Industry, she turned over part of her payment to cover the scholarship she had received in 1893. No one expected repayment,

PIERRE AND MARIE CURIE AT WORK TOGETHER IN THE LAB.

but Marie felt that the money would contribute to the education of another Polish student. "Having grown up in an atmosphere of patriotism kept alive by the oppression of Poland, I wished, like many other young people of my country, to contribute my effort toward the conservation of our national spirit," she later said.[7]

In September 1897, the Curies' first child, Irène, was born—delivered by Pierre's father. Soon after, Pierre's mother died of breast cancer, and Dr. Curie moved with his son, daughter-in-law, and granddaughter into a house on the outskirts of Paris. The Curies took on hired help to see to household chores. Marie's father-in-law proved himself an able babysitter for Irène, and Marie was able leave the child with him while she worked.

Marie and Pierre also maintained close ties with Jacques and his wife, though they did not often see one another. Marie still missed her own family in Poland, especially after Bronya returned there with her husband; nevertheless, she was leading a satisfying and rewarding life. "It was under this mode of quiet living, organized according to our desires, that we achieved the great work of our lives, work begun about the end of 1897 and lasting for many years," she later wrote.[8]

Marie's next challenge was choosing a topic for her doctoral research—a daunting task, considering that at the time, no woman had ever received a doctorate in science in any country. Two years earlier, a German physicist named Wilhelm Röntgen had discovered a kind of "ray" that was able to travel through solids and provide "photographs" of the bones of living people. He called it an X-ray, the X signifying an unknown. (For his discovery, Röntgen would become the first Nobel Prize winner in physics in 1901).

Shortly after Röntgen's discovery, Henri Becquerel, a French scientist, discovered that uranium compounds emit a kind of ray that "fogs" a photographic plate, even if the compounds are kept out of the light. Becquerel's discovery did not receive as much attention in the general scientific community as Röntgen's X-rays, but Marie Curie found Becquerel's findings more interesting. She persuaded the director of the school where Pierre worked to supply her with room to test her theories on the uranium rays—and a musty, cramped storeroom became her laboratory. Using an instrument that Pierre and Jacques invented years earlier,

Marie measured the barely detectable electrical currents that pass through the air when it is subjected to uranium rays. Eventually she was able to confirm Becquerel's findings that uranium, in any form and under any conditions, emits constant rays, and that minerals containing a higher amount of uranium emit stronger rays than those with lower amounts. With Pierre's help she went further, hypothesizing that the rays emitted by uranium were actually a property of the element itself, and that this quality was part of uranium's atomic structure. It was a simple hypothesis, but it forever changed the way physicists viewed the basic building block of matter, the atom.

Scientists of the time were just learning that the atom was not the most elementary particle in the universe, that it consisted of even smaller particles. This was proved with the recent discovery of the electron. But physicists did not yet understand the atom's structure or what was responsible for its energy. At first, Marie and Pierre did not believe that the "rays" coming from uranium originated within the atom. Perhaps, they first theorized, such rays were "caught" from an outside source by uranium atoms and then radiated out of the atom.

On February 17, 1898, however, Marie tested a heavy, black, tarry material known as pitchblende, from which the element of uranium was discovered and later mined. To her surprise, pitchblende produced an even stronger electrical current than uranium alone. For the next few days, a puzzled Marie continued testing pitchblende, pure uranium, and several uranium compounds. Soon after, she discovered that a mineral called aeschynite, which contains thorium but no uranium, also produced a stronger current than uranium alone.

By April, she began to believe that the uranium "rays" were not a property of that element in particular, but rather were a sign of a broader phenomenon that had not yet been explored. To describe the behavior of uranium and thorium, Marie devised the word *radioactivity*, based on the Latin word for "ray."

Pierre had grown so intrigued by Marie's work that he began collaborating with her. With the goal of tracking down the new radioactive elements that seemed to emit stronger rays than uranium, Marie continued testing pitchblende—a substance consisting of as many as thirty different elements. The Curies became the first scientists to use a new method of chemical analysis. They used several standard methods to separate different types of chemical substances, and then used radiation measurements to "trace" the tiny amounts of unknown radioactive elements among the "fractions" that resulted.

They discovered that the two most radioactive fractions in pitchblende contained bismuth and barium. In July 1898 they published their conclusion that the bismuth fraction actually contained a new element, which they named polonium in honor of Marie's homeland. Six months later, in a second published report, they announced their discovery of a second new element, found in the barium fraction. They named this element radium.

The next step was to convince other scientists that polonium and radium actually existed, and then to identify and describe the nature of the new elements. Marie moved her lab to an abandoned building across the courtyard from the

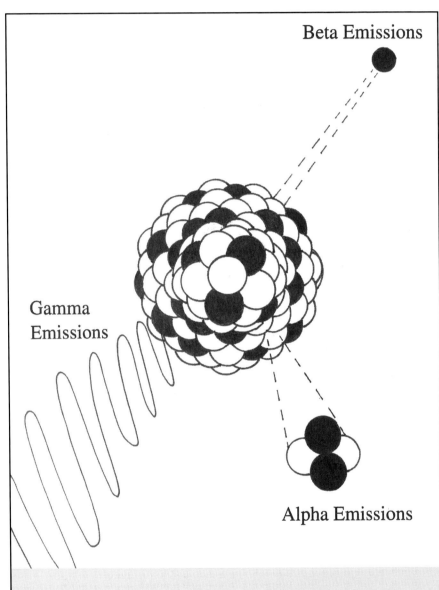

Beta Emissions

Gamma
Emissions

Alpha Emissions

RADIOACTIVE SUBSTANCES MAY EMIT RADIATION IN THREE DIFFERENT
FORMS: AS ALPHA PARTICLES, BETA PARTICLES, OR GAMMA RAYS.

tiny storeroom in which she had been working, and set out to isolate the new elements from the bismuth and barium. To do so, she had to treat huge amounts of pitchblende, which were supplied by Austrian mines eager to see whether she could find a use for their otherwise unusable by-products. A firm called the Central Chemical Products Company helped the Curies treat the pitchblende by adapting the Curies' laboratory techniques to a large-scale process, in exchange for which they were given a share of the radium salts that resulted.

For three years, Marie and Pierre worked to separate the radium from the barium. Finally, she isolated one-tenth of a gram of pure radium chloride. By 1903, scientists learned that radioactive materials "decay," which explained why Marie Curie failed to isolate polonium.

In 1902, the French Academy of Sciences nominated Henri Becquerel and Pierre Curie—but not Marie Curie—for the new and prestigious Nobel Prize in Physics for their work in radioactivity. Magnus Gösta Mittag-Leffler, a Swedish mathematician on the Nobel nominating committee and an advocate of women in the sciences, wrote immediately to Pierre to inform him of the situation. Pierre insisted that any Nobel Prize for research in radioactivity that did not include recognition of Marie Curie's role would be pointless. After much deliberation and behind-the-scenes help from colleagues, Marie's 1902 nomination was validated for the 1903 prize. If not for Mittag-Leffler, she might never have been officially recognized for her groundbreaking work.

CHAPTER FIVE

A PATH SHAPED OUT OF TRAGEDY

Receiving the Nobel Prize in 1903 caused great upheaval in the lives of the Curies. With international acclaim came enormous loss of privacy—and thus a loss of family and research time. Marie Curie would later describe this time as "serious trouble," but added, "Of course, people who contribute to that kind of trouble generally mean it kindly."[1] Although she appreciated the praise and attention, much of it appeared to be less about the scientific work that had earned the award and more about the "romance" of winning it. More disturbing were the constant interruptions and intrusions by journalists and other "well-wishers." In a letter to Georges Gouy that year, Pierre angrily wrote:

> We have been pursued by journalists and photographers from all the countries of the world, they have gone so far as to reproduce the conversation of my daughter with her

maid and to describe the black and white cat who lives with us. Then we have received letters and visits from all the eccentrics, from all the unknown inventors, and from all the unknowns in general—then we have had requests for money in great numbers, and finally collectors of autographs, snobs, worldly people and even sometimes people of science have come to see us in the magnificent setting of rue Lhomond with which you are familiar. With all that, not an instant of tranquillity in the laboratory and a voluminous correspondence to take care of every evening. With this routine, I feel mindlessness invading me.[2]

Another difficulty for the Curies was Pierre's increasingly poor health. In June 1903, both the Curies had been invited to London, England, as guests of the prestigious Royal Institution. Custom did not allow women lecturers, so only Pierre delivered a description of their work at his "Friday Evening Discourse," making sure to credit Marie's vital role in their work. However, Pierre was feeling so ill from his rheumatism that he could barely dress himself before his lecture. His hands were so covered with sores that, while demonstrating radium's properties in his talk, he accidentally spilled some of it.

The additional income from the Nobel Prize might have allowed Marie to stop teaching at Sèvres, but she chose to continue. She derived great enjoyment from the work, in part because many of her students reminded her of herself when she was younger. "These pupils were girls of about twenty years who had entered the school after severe examination," she later wrote, "and [they] had still to work very seriously to meet the requirements that would enable them to be named professors in the lycées." All of them, she maintained, "worked with great eagerness, and it was a pleasure for me to direct their studies in physics."[3]

Because Marie had had little experience when she began teaching at Sèvres, her first year was difficult. By her second year, however, she had earned the respect of her fellow professors and her students. One of her early students, Lucienne Goss Fabin, went on to become a professor herself. She described Marie Curie's courses at Sèvres as "the essential reference during the entire length of my career. She didn't dazzle us, she reassured us, attracted us, held us with her simplicity, her desire to be useful to us, the sense she had of both our ignorance and our possibilities."[4]

One of the differences between Marie's classes and those of the other professors, said another student, was that Madame Curie insisted on using the instruments in the school's classrooms to give the students hands-on experience. At times she brought in equipment that she had developed or modified herself. She had invited her class to attend her dissertation defense in June 1903, and once even took them to Pierre's laboratory on Rue Cuvier to meet her husband and observe his attempts to measure the quantity of heat given off by radium. She then coaxed them to re-create his experiment in their school labs. Were it not for Marie Curie, the students at Sèvres might have believed that all one could learn about physics could be gleaned from books alone.

In August of a very hectic 1904, the Curies took a much-needed family vacation. They chose to spend it a quiet farmhouse in the village of St.-Rémy-les-Chevreuse, about an hour's train ride from Paris. The relatively short traveling distance allowed Pierre to continue concentrating on his

THIS FAMOUS CARICATURE OF THE CURIES, "RADIUM," FIRST RAN IN THE POPULAR BRITISH PERIODICAL *VANITY FAIR*.

work but still spend a bit of time with the family. Marie, on the other hand, developed a growing desire to spend more time at home. By the time the Curies departed for their vacation, she was five months pregnant. Having miscarried in the fifth month of her second pregnancy the previous August (possibly from exposure to radioactivity), she was determined to take every precaution to avoid another loss. The farm at St. Rémy provided respite from the stress of work and media attention, but the Curies were still close enough to Paris doctors so that Marie felt secure should any problems arise with her pregnancy.

For Pierre, the farm was a refreshing retreat. St. Rémy, located a few miles south of his childhood home, was familiar to him and helped him rally from his illness and his disappointment that his work was progressing so slowly as a result of his health problems. As an added treat, Pierre's brother, Jacques Curie, his wife, and their two children also accompanied Marie, Pierre, and Iréne to St. Rémy.

The Curies' second child, Eve Denise, was born on December 6, 1904, after a difficult birth and a long "lying in" period, during which Marie struggled mightily with depression. Not only was Pierre's health deteriorating—he would sometimes remain awake all night, unable to sleep from almost unbearable pain—but Marie herself seemed to have lost all enthusiasm for science, her own home life, and even for the child who was about to be born. She expressed her feelings to her sister Bronya, who, having lost her second child the year before to tubercular meningitis, traveled from Poland for her sister's delivery. "Why am I bringing this creature into the world?" lamented Marie. "Existence is too hard, too barren. We ought not to inflict it on innocent ones."[5]

Once Eve was born, however, Marie felt nothing but delight at her birth. As with Irène, Marie kept careful records of her youngest child's progress, but in Eve's case they were usually observations of behavior, not physical growth. At the same time, Marie kept careful watch over her eldest daughter. Not only was Irène in the throes of the usual sibling jealousy over a new baby, but she was also, like her father, prone to health problems. In 1904, the child contracted whooping cough and had several cases of unexplained fever; another illness turned out to be scarlet fever. With the help of Pierre's father, a nanny, a maid, and a wet nurse, Marie managed to handle the challenges of her growing family and to return to her laboratory and teaching work after a brief absence.

In July 1905, Pierre was at last elected to the French Academy of Science, having just slightly edged ahead of another candidate, M. Gernez. The division of votes rankled Pierre. In a letter to George Gouy dated July 24, he wrote, "I find myself in the Academy without having desired to be there and without the Academy's desire to have me. . . . [E]verybody told me it was agreed that I would have fifty votes. That's probably why I nearly didn't get in!"[6] Additionally, though Pierre was offered a coveted position of a chair in physics at the Sorbonne, he might have to forfeit the right to have his own lab. This meant he might not be able to continue his work at all. He wrote a polite but firm letter to the Sorbonne, explaining that he would be forced to give up the position offered him if it did not include a laboratory or financial provisions to continue his work. After more rounds of bargaining, the Sorbonne agreed to give him two rooms off the campus on Rue Cuvier, and an appropriation of monies that was less than generous. A more generous offer of working room and money by a wealthy would-be patroness came to nothing. Not until much later was Marie Curie able to establish a laboratory befitting the couple's momentous discovery and their continued research.

In June 1905, when Pierre was feeling stronger and the attention from the press seemed to die down, the Curies decided it was time to fulfill a duty they'd postponed several times—delivering the Nobel Prize lecture in Stockholm, Sweden. The Curies made the journey, and Pierre spoke on the consequences of their discovery of radium before the Academy of Sciences of Stockholm. As his daughter Eve would explain years later:

> In physics [the discovery] profoundly modified the fundamental principles of mechanics. In chemistry it stirred up bold hypotheses on the source of energy which supplied the radioactive phenomena. In geology, in meteorology, it was the key to phenomena which had never been explained before. In biology, last of all, the action of radium on cancerous cells had proved efficacious. Radium had enriched Knowledge and served the Good. But could it also serve Evil?[7]

Pierre took great pains to emphasize that in the wrong hands, the powerful effects of radium could be extremely dangerous. "Here we may ask ourselves if humanity has anything to gain by learning the secrets of nature," he said, "if it is ripe enough to profit by them, or if this knowledge is not harmful."[8] Using Nobel's own discovery of "powerful

MARIE CURIE'S DAUGHTERS, EVE AND IRÈNE.

explosives," he noted that in addition to great benefits, the discovery also brought the greater possibility of "a terrible means of destruction" in the hands of the wrong people. He concluded optimistically, "I am among those who think, with Nobel, that humanity will obtain more good than evil from the new discoveries."[9]

Pierre did manage to draw a victory from his struggle for research monies. In November 1905, he was informed that he was to be given three coworkers for his research: a chief of laboratory work, a laboratory assistant, and a lab aid. He chose Marie as his chief of laboratory work. For the first time, Marie had established herself as an official worker in her husband's labs, complete with a yearly salary of 2,400 francs.

By early April 1906, life seemed to be looking up for the Curies. The family took an Easter vacation at St. Rémy, and there Pierre reveled in the efforts of eight-year-old Irène as she attempted to catch butterflies in a net, and laughed at the comical seriousness with which fourteen-month-old Eve tried to stay on two feet in the ridged tracks left in the road by carts. The weather was excellent, and the Curies spent their leisure time fetching milk at a nearby farm, riding their bicycles in the woods, and stretching out to cool off in a grassy meadow while they watched Irène and Eve play nearby. Pierre was feeling much better physically, and he was happy to be going back to work in earnest. He left earlier than the rest of the family to return to his laboratory; the following day, April 18, Marie brought the children back to Paris and joined Pierre in the lab. That night, the Curies attended a dinner held by the Physical Society, and Pierre discussed with Henri Poincaré some of the issues that had lately been on his mind, including how to measure the emanation of radium, how he intended to educate his children in the natural sciences, and the experiment in spiritism that he had recently attended. As the Curies made their way home, the weather turned from balmy to blustery, and a heavy rain began to fall.

On Thursday, April 19, 1906, Pierre had a full schedule. He planned to attend a luncheon of the Association of Professors in the Faculty of Science at the Hôtel des Sociétés Savantes on Rue Danton, and then he had an appointment to review proofs with his publisher, Gauthier-Villars. He also intended to make a trip to a nearby library, and was going to stop in at the Institute. That evening, he would be entertaining fellow scientists at the Curie home. Marie, busy with the children that morning, barely saw her husband. He called upstairs to ask whether she would be going to the laboratory that day; she replied that she would most likely not have time.

Pierre never made it to the library that day. After working in his lab throughout the morning, he made his way across the city in the driving rain to attend the luncheon. There, he spoke strongly about the necessity of broadening career options for new faculty and putting in place specific laws and regulations to govern laboratory work and prevent accidents. After the meeting ended, he again ventured out in the rain, this time to see his publisher. When he arrived, however, he found that the building was locked because of a workers' strike.

Pierre Curie left his publisher and hurried down Rue Dauphine, a very crowded, narrow street, along which ran even narrower sidewalks. Lost in thought, Pierre sought the edge of the street rather than the sidewalk itself, so that he would have more room to move. He was following a closed cab.

At the corner of Rue Dauphine and the Quai, a horse-drawn lorry cut across and entered Rue Dauphine at a trot. Distracted, Pierre decided to cross the road to the sidewalk on the other side, and stepped out from behind the cab. At that moment, the six-ton lorry, loaded with military uniforms, thundered by in the opposite direction. Pierre had turned directly into the path of the horses. Surprised, he lost his footing on the wet pavement and attempted to grab the animals' harness, but instead he slipped to the ground.

Even then Pierre Curie might have survived—he had miraculously missed being struck by the horses' hooves and the front wheels of the lorry—but the left rear wheel, with its enormous weight, crushed Pierre's head. He died instantly.

Policemen retrieved the body and discovered who it was; a crowd that had gathered around the accident began threatening the driver of the lorry and grew so violent that other police officers had to protect him. Pierre Curie's body was taken to a nearby police station, where a doctor examined him. Curie's laboratory assistant, Pierre Clerc, tearfully identified the body. The police notified the Association of Professors first, as Clerc and the sobbing lorry driver stood by.

"What was he dreaming of this time?" Pierre's heartbroken father asked again and again when told the terrible news of his son's death.[10] Even Clerc was certain that the physicist was probably deep in thought and thus distracted while crossing the street.

Marie did not immediately learn the devastating news. When a representative of the President of the Republic arrived at the Curies' front door, Marie was not in. He left without delivering the sad news. Paul Appell, the dean of the Sorbonne faculty, and another professor arrived at the house shortly after; they also learned that Marie was not in. Although Pierre's father was there, the dean had been told to deliver the news to Marie first, and he hesitated. Dr. Curie looked at the stricken faces of his visitors and knew what they had come for. "My son is dead," he said simply.

Marie arrived home at about six o'clock that evening, and like her father-in-law knew when she saw the visitors' faces that something terrible had happened. The dean once again gave the details of the accident. Marie stood motionless as she took in the news. Finally she said, "Pierre is dead? Dead? Absolutely dead?"

Years later, Eve Curie would describe what she believed happened to her mother at the moment when she learned her husband had died:

> Marie Curie did not change from a happy young wife to an inconsolable widow. The metamorphosis was less simple and more serious. The interior tumult that lacerated Marie, the nameless horror of her wandering ideas, were too virulent to be expressed in complaints or in confidences. From the moment when those three words, "Pierre is dead," reached her consciousness, a cope of solitude and secrecy fell upon her shoulders forever. Mme. Curie, on that day in April, became not only a widow, but at the same time a pitiful and incurably lonely woman.[11]

Despite Marie's deep shock and grief, she immediately

began attending to funeral arrangements for her husband. She sent Irène to stay with a neighbor for a few days. Next, she sent news of Pierre's death to her relatives in Poland via a brief telegram. (Her sister Bronya arrived soon after receiving word.) Marie refused an autopsy and asked officials to have the body returned to the house. Only when Pierre's brother Jacques arrived the following day from Montpellier did Marie break down.

The news of his death traveled around the world, and once again—although for very different reasons—the Curie household was swamped with letters and telegrams. Messages from "kings, ministers, poets and scientists" arrived, "mixed with [letters of sympathy from] obscure names," Eve Curie wrote many years later.[12] Marie, who as usual wished to avoid the hubbub and formalities of an official ceremony to honor Pierre, decided to move up the date of the funeral to April 21, just two days after her husband's death. She refused to allow processions, speeches, and official delegations. Aristide Briand, the minister of public instruction, nevertheless accompanied the small band of mourners to a small cemetery in Sceaux, on the outskirts of Paris. There, Pierre Curie was buried near his mother in the Curie family plot.

One of the ways in which Jacques Curie helped his sister-in-law deal with her grief was to encourage her to return to work in the laboratory as soon as possible. Marie took the advice and was back at work on April 22, the day after the funeral. "Crushed by the blow, I did not feel able to face the future," she said. "I could not forget, however, what my husband used to say, that even deprived of him, I ought to continue my work."[13] But when Jacques told

Marie that the French government was offering to support her and the children with a state pension, she refused immediately. She was perfectly able to support her family, she maintained.

Less than a month after Pierre's death, however, Marie received an offer from the Sorbonne to assume her husband's academic post. This time, Marie accepted. She believed that doing so was the best way to fulfill Pierre's—and her—dream of establishing a state-of-the-art laboratory. She was determined to create a full scientific institution in memory of Pierre. On May 13, 1906, the council of the Association of Professors officially decided to maintain the chair created for Pierre Curie and to give it to Marie, who was given the title *chargée de cours*. It marked the first time in France's history that a woman was given such a position in higher education. She remembered Pierre's words: "Whatever happens, even if one has to go on like a body without a soul, one must work just the same."[14] In her diary, in a letter to her late husband, she told him the news. "I have been named to your chair," she wrote, "and . . . there have been some imbeciles to congratulate me on it."[15]

Despite the devastating loss of Pierre, Marie found some solace in continuing their work. The following spring, she found and rented a new home for herself and her daughters at 6 Rue du Chemin De Fer in Sceaux. The move required her to take a daily half-hour train ride to and from the laboratory, but the small house had a garden for the children to enjoy. She hired a distant relative from Poland to act as governess and housekeeper, and Pierre's father stayed with them. His presence was a comfort both to

Marie and her children; he was especially close with Iréne. When he died in February 1910 after being bedridden for a year with lung congestion, Marie and the children were again devastated. She had Pierre's coffin disinterred briefly so that she could place the coffin of her father-in-law beneath him in the ground. An empty space above Pierre was meant for her; she did not want to be separated from her late husband even in death.

Within three years of Pierre Curie's death, Marie had expanded the laboratory they once shared. The number of workers in the lab grew from seven to twenty-four. With funds from the Carnegie Foundation (established by American steel magnate Andrew Carnegie), Marie offered stipends to promising researchers from around the world. She also convinced the University of Paris and the Pasteur Institute to commit to financing a laboratory to suit her needs and specifications. This, at long last, was the facility that had been promised to Pierre—the Radium Institute.

HARSH JUDGMENT AND RENEWAL

Too busy to handle all of her responsibilities after the founding of the Radium Institute, Marie turned over her post at the Sèvres school to her friend and colleague, Paul Langevin. Langevin first met Pierre Curie in 1888, when the sixteen-year-old attended the *École de physique et chimie* to study under Curie. He took over Pierre's job when the professor left the school in 1904. Langevin and Marie taught together at the Sèvres before he assumed her post in 1906 when Marie accepted Pierre's academic post at the Sorbonne. Pierre thought highly of the young man; in a letter to Georges Gouy he had praised Langevin's energy: "[He] is standing in for Mascart at the College, my wife at Sévres [when she was ill] and me at the École de physique; what's more he has a family, numerous students and he has been preparing a number of papers."[1] Moreover, Pierre Curie observed that Langevin believed in the existence of electrons and was quite knowledgeable on the topic. Pierre found Langevin an admirable, hard-working scientist, praising him as one of the best physicists at the École de physique.

Langevin was deeply grieved over the loss of his colleague and mentor. In the year after Pierre's death, the thirty-five-year-old scientist made what would come to be known as his most important scientific contribution: he applied electron theory to the phenomena of magnetism, synthesizing the ideas of Pierre Curie and another mentor, J. J. Thomson. It did not take long for the enthusiastic scientist to become close friends with Marie Curie. Marie became a confidante for Langevin. Long aware that his

THE PARIS RADIUM INSTITUTE.

marriage was under some strain, he had admitted to some friends that he had contemplated divorce. However, his concern always shifted from his own unhappiness to worries about how a divorce would affect his four children.

Marie Curie and Paul Langevin became close friends—so close that some historians believe they eventually had a romantic affair. The beliefs were based on evidence that they shared a rented apartment and that their letters to one another were filled with affection and devotion. The situation was made even worse by the fact that Langevin's wife, Jeanne, was a violent and unstable woman. She had become openly jealous of Marie Curie, even though the Curies and Langevins had been friendly when Pierre was alive. Jeanne Langevin ultimately threatened to do physical harm to Marie Curie and to expose her alleged affair with Paul. Ultimately, the two scientists agreed to stop meeting, even for scientific study.

In September of 1910, however, shortly after the incident with Jeanne Langevin, Marie and Paul traveled with another colleague and friend, Jean Perrin, to the International Congress of Radiology and Electricity in Brussels. Almost immediately, Marie became quite ill, and she remained so throughout most of the congress. Still, the meeting was a great success: its most important outcome was establishing an international standard for radium. A committee whose members included the most pre-eminent researchers of Europe and the United States (including Marie herself) voted to award Marie the responsibility of preparing a sample of 20 milligrams of pure radium. Marie would keep the radium sample in Paris. This new unit of measurement (the amount of radium emanation equal to one gram of radium) was eventually given the name "curie," in honor of Pierre.

Marie's domestic troubles did not end upon her return home. Paul Langevin's wife was still making threats against her. Finally, Marie decided to take a much-needed vacation with her family. Marie's sister Helena and Helena's daughter Hania were visiting from Poland. They accompanied Irène and Eve to the tiny Brittany coast community of L'Arcouëst where Marie arranged to meet up with them. When she arrived, Marie was drained, pensive, and still ailing.

The respite away from the Langevin controversy and crushing workload did wonders for Marie. Her spirits were further lifted on her return to Paris in the fall of 1910. After her much deserved rest, some of her colleagues began suggesting that Marie consider becoming a candidate to fill the physics chair in the Academy of Sciences. The chair opened as a result of the death of chemist and physicist Désiré Gernez in October.

Marie's friends made a good argument for her candidacy—she was one of three living Nobel Prize winners in France, but the only one not yet to become a member of the Institute. Marie was also a crucial member of the International Radium Standard Committee and held memberships in the Swedish, Dutch, Czech, and Polish Academies, as well as the American Philosophical Society and the Imperial Academy in St. Petersburg, Russia. Some viewed not inviting Marie into the French Academy a slight and an embarrassment to a well-respected fellow scientist.

No legal stipulations prevented a woman from becoming a member of the French Academy. However, Marie was not aware of "the antagonism her strong personality aroused in

MARIE CURIE AND HER DAUGHTERS, EVE AND IRÈNE.

certain quarters . . . not to mention the horror many felt at her brazen attempt to storm the last male bastion remaining in her field."[2] Still, after seeking the opinion of Pierre's friend Georges Gouy, and weighing the advantages of sitting on such a prestigious post, Marie submitted her name for consideration. Even though the press had hounded Marie and Pierre during their life together, coverage of the two was nearly always complimentary. However, when Marie announced her candidacy for the physics chair at the Academy, she suddenly had a host of adversaries and was facing a fierce rival.

Marie's biggest challenger for the physics chair was a sixty-seven-year-old scientist named Edouard Branly. He and Marie Curie had shared the Prix Osiris in 1903. Perhaps more importantly years earlier, in 1889, Branly had worked with recently discovered radio waves, finding that it was possible to create radio communication without wire to direct the current. He called his invention a "coherer," which was vital to Guglielmo Marconi's establishing wireless communication between Bologna, Italy, and Douvres, France later that same year. A relatively modest man, Branly nevertheless had many allies, including the conservative clerics of the Catholic Church. It did not hurt that Branly himself was a teacher at the Catholic Institute.

Support for Branly grew even greater when in 1909 Marconi—and not Branly—won the Nobel Prize for the experiments with radio waves. Against Branly, said Gouy, were the "university elements of the Academy, which will hardly forgive him for having abandoned the Sorbonne some time ago for the Catholic Faculty. And then, he wrote

Marie, "his work has little in it to compare to your qualifications."[3]

The clerics-versus-academics issue did figure into the debate over whether Curie or Branly should be named, but another issue loomed even larger: if elected, Marie would become the first female member of the 215-year-old institution. The press covered the "historic election" angle relentlessly in the month between her nomination and the actual vote. Marie had hoped, and perhaps had even expected the debate to center on the actual merits of her candidacy. Unfortunately, the press coverage focused on the "symbolism" of electing a woman, the divisions between church and government, and the difference between electing a "foreigner" (like Marie Curie) and a "real" native of France (like Branly).

Marie's supporters tried to offset the extraneous arguments against her by stressing her scientific accomplishments and the importance of her research. Sorbonne Faculty of Sciences dean Jean-Gaston Darboux wrote to one newspaper that Marie Curie had, for the past fourteen years, "pursued with tireless ardor, either alone or with her husband, an admirable number of research projects."[4] And to those who might believe that she was a mere assistant to her husband, Darboux added that in Pierre's Nobel Prize presentation he included a "touching testament" to her accomplishments. He pointed out that she had only recently isolated radium in its pure state and produced two volumes [the *Traité de radioactivité*] of reviews of current research—not only of her own but of her colleagues and collaborators.

On January 24, 1911, after much additional debate, the

Academy took a final vote on who would fill Gernez's chair. The decision was deemed so volatile that extra guards were posted around the Institute. At first, only Academy of Sciences members were admitted inside, but eventually president Gautier allowed outsiders to enter—except women, who were traditionally barred from entering the Institute.

After the first, Marie had tallied twenty-eight, Branly twenty-nine, and the other contender Marcel Brillouin, one. Since there was no clear majority, another vote was taken, with Marie retaining her twenty-eight votes. However, Brillouin's vote went to Branly giving him thirty, and he was named the new chair at the Academy. Marie's own reaction to the Academy's decision was hardly noticeable. Just as she disliked being the center of attention after she and Pierre won the Nobel Prize in 1903, she was more disturbed by the ways in which her name and character had been taken up by journalists who knew nothing about her, and very little about her work. Marie received the news of the election via a telephone call in her small office at the Rue Cuvier. Her staff was prepared to offer words of comfort when she emerged from the office, but as Eve Curie wrote about her mother's reaction, "She was not to comment by so much as a word upon this setback which . . . afflicted her," returning to her work as if it was business as usual.[5]

The press had not yet finished with Marie Curie, however. In the summer of 1911, word of her alleged affair with Paul Langevin reached the press. Jeanne Langevin apparently had possession of letters written between Marie and Paul that appeared to confirm an affair, and she set out to ruin Marie's reputation. In turn, Marie once again sought the advice of her longtime friend, Jean Perrin, and told him about the threat. Perrin suggested she leave the country for a time, and she arranged to travel to Genoa, Italy, with her children in the company of mathematician Emile Borel and his wife, Marguerite, who were scheduled to attend a scientific conference.

Back in Paris, the problems in the Langevin marriage came to a head, and Paul eventually took his two oldest sons and left for a month's vacation. Claiming he had intended to take the vacation all along, he nevertheless notified his brother-in-law that he was leaving and then consulted an attorney to be sure that his departure would not jeopardize his case in the event he and his wife divorced.

Jeanne Langevin, who did not learn that her husband and two children were gone until the following day, also consulted an attorney and charged her husband with abandonment. While he returned the children to his wife's care, he was constantly concerned that his wife would release the contents of the letters and ruin Marie's reputation.

At the end of October 1911, Marie left Paris once again to attend the first Solvay Conference in Brussels. The conference, named after the Brussels manufacturer and chemist who developed a new process for producing sodium, would become an important event in the field of physics. Ernest Solvay had learned about the quantum theories of Max Planck and Albert Einstein, and with a German colleague named Walter Nernst, he developed a plan for a conference to discuss the issue. Twenty-one European and English scientists and at least five French scientists, including Marie Curie, Paul Langevin, and Jean Perrin, attended the first

ALBERT EINSTEIN (ABOVE) GREATLY ADMIRED MARIE CURIE'S
INTELLIGENCE AND PASSION FOR SCIENCE.

conference. Although Marie did not present a paper, she did participate in the lively discussions. Einstein later reported that she also socialized with the other attendees, and he was drawn to what he called her "passionateness" and "sparkling intelligence." He later wrote, "I spent much time together with Jean Perrin, Paul Langevin, and Madame Curie, and I am just delighted with these people. The latter even promised me to visit us with her daughters."[6]

While the conference was still in progress, the story of the presumed affair between Marie Curie and Paul Langevin broke. A writer from the *Journal* apparently spoke with Jeanne Langevin's mother, who supplied him with enough half-truths to create a scandalous story for the newspaper. The reporter intimated in his November 4 article that when Paul left with his two oldest children some months before, he had also taken along Marie Curie. He also claimed that at present, Paul's wife did not know where he was—and no one knew where Marie Curie was, either.

Marie learned about the report and in a handwritten note she denied the allegations, calling them "pure fantasy," and added, "It is well known in Paris where I could be found."[7] Despite her protests, the story was picked up and embellished upon by several other newspapers. Finally, four days after the initial story appeared in the *Journal*, Marie had had enough. Along with a retraction by the reporter who wrote the original story, she arranged for yet another statement in her own defense to be published in *le Temps*:

I consider abominable the entire intrusion of the press and the public into private life. This intrusion is particularly criminal when it involves people who have manifestly consecrated their life to preoccupations of an elevated order and general utility. . . . There is nothing in my acts which obliges me to feel diminished. I will not add anything. . . . But from now on I will rigorously pursue all publication of writings which are attributed to me or tendentious allegations regarding me. Since I have the right, I will demand damages and interest of considerable sums which will be used in the interests of science.[8]

Ironically, just one day before Marie Curie's second letter appeared, newspapers were also informed that she had been awarded the Nobel Prize in chemistry for 1911. Cited in the November 7 announcement were Marie's successes in discovering the radioactive elements, obtaining a sample of radium that was pure enough to establish the element's atomic weight, and obtaining radium in a metallic state. The Curies' discovery of induced radioactivity in 1899, the report said, had allowed Ernest Rutherford and others to study emanations and the disintegration theory. Additionally, the Nobel Prize committee noted that the possibility now existed that radium could be used as a treatment for cancer.

Although the Swedish Academy knew about the scandal involving Marie, it had investigated and found the rumors to be groundless. But French journalists were less forgiving. Very few reported on Marie's second Nobel Prize, or they buried the story in the back pages. Once again, Marie's supporters, who now included Albert Einstein, rallied to her defense and flooded the French newspapers with letters protesting her mistreatment at their hands.

When Marie returned to France only to find an angry mob of people gathered in front of her Sceaux home, she immediately took badly frightened Irène, now fourteen, and Eve, now seven, to the home of her friend Emile Borel. Despite threats that he would be fired for "sullying French academic honor," Borel refused to deny the Curies shelter. Meanwhile, Langevin and a journalist who had sullied Marie's reputation held a duel that, while emotional, was entirely bloodless.

The good news that Marie had won a second Nobel Prize failed to diminish the pressure of the constant attention by journalists and the damage to her public reputation. Marie's health had begun to deteriorate from the stress of the intrusion into her private life and the long hours she spent working. Still, as ill and frail as she was, Marie made the forty-eight hour journey to Stockholm in December 1911 to accept her Nobel award. Understandably concerned about Marie's ill health, Bronya and Irène accompanied the frail scientist to Sweden. She stood in the great Hall of Prizes in the Royal Palace to accept the Nobel Prize from King Gustav V, and memories of her beloved Pierre flooded back to her.

The stress finally took its toll. Already suffering from severe depression, Marie also developed a kidney ailment that eventually required surgery. While beset by this illness, she hid herself from the public.[9] While she recuperated— first at a little house near Paris, and that summer at the home of her friend, Hertha Ayrton, in England—Marie traveled under the name "Dluska."

During her recuperation Marie received a visit from a delegation of Polish professors who appealed to her to return to her native Poland to head up a new radioactivity laboratory in Warsaw. The idea was to "bring the greatest woman scientist in the world back to her fatherland."[10]

Marie felt torn between returning to her homeland and jeopardizing the construction of the Radium Institute in Paris. She ultimately turned down the Warsaw offer, but agreed to offer direction from afar.

Marie returned to her Paris apartment in October 1912, and two months later she returned to the laboratory to continue her work. She made the trip to Warsaw in 1913 for the inauguration of the radioactivity building. A highlight of the trip was attending one of the ceremonies in the Museum of Industry and Agriculture, where twenty-two years before Marie had conducted her first physics experiments. When she returned to Paris, the Langevin scandal was for the most part old news, and Marie Curie was determined to devote as much time as she could to her ongoing research and oversee the completion of the Radium Institute.

CHAPTER SEVEN

INNOVATION AT THE BATTLEFRONT

The Radium Institute was completed at a time of great political upheaval in Europe. On August 4, 1914, Germany declared war on France. Although most French citizens seemed to express optimism about the outcome of war, Marie Curie knew from her experiences in Poland that France was in for a long and difficult battle. "It is hard to think that, after so many centuries of development, the human race still doesn't know how to resolve difficulties in any way except by violence," she wrote to her daughter, Irène.[1] Marie was also determined to make a significant contribution to the war effort in her adopted homeland, recognizing that national interests would certainly take priority over scientific endeavors.

News of the impending war emptied Paris of Marie's male students and colleagues, who joined or were recruited into the military. As a result, all work at the Radium Institute was put on hold. Every able-bodied citizen was channeling his or her energies into helping France win the war. In August Marie learned that Germany was occupying her beloved Poland. At month's end, most middle-class Parisians had abandoned the city, and the government itself had moved its headquarters to Bordeaux. Yet Marie Curie remained, believing that she must stay at her "post."

In early September of 1914, Paris felt the full force of war as German bombs began rocking the city. One of Marie's first actions was to move the Institute's supply of radium out of Paris: a government decree had declared the radium in her possession "a national treasure of inestimable value," and Marie was ordered to transport it to Bordeaux for safekeeping.[2] On September 3, she carried the radium, encased in lead, onto the train to Bordeaux, accompanied by a government agent. The following day, on a train crowded with soldiers and few civilians Marie returned to Paris, relieved to learn that the French and British forces had turned back the Germany army. For the time being, Paris would not be invaded.

Rather than "become, like a great many courageous Frenchwomen, a nurse in white veils," Marie set out to find out where she could best assist with the needs of the Medical service.[3] She did not have to look long before discovering that hospitals, both on the front lines as well as behind the front were without sufficient X-ray equipment. The X-ray, a discovery of Wilhelm Röntgen in 1895, presented doctors with the capability to see inside the human body and photograph its bones. Much to Marie's dismay, only a few of Röntgen's X-ray machines were available in

1914, and they were relegated to large medical centers. Recognizing the tremendous benefits X-ray technology would provide in the diagnosis and treatment of the wounded, Marie created mobile radiology centers that would provide X-ray services for French soldiers.

As the newly named Director of the Red Cross Radiology Service, Marie convinced the city's auto repair shops to convert motor cars into medical vans. She used equipment that lay unused in laboratories to construct X-ray machines, and had the auto mechanics mount them to motor cars so that they could be easily transported to front-line hospitals. The machines were operated using electricity generated by the engines of the motor cars; they could also take advantage of available electricity at the hospitals.

Marie also elicited promises of help and donations of equipment from numerous businesses and manufacturers. By October 1914, she had amassed twenty radiology vehicles—dubbed *petit Curies*—that were ready for service at the front lines of the war. She taught herself how to drive, learned basic auto mechanics, and studied anatomy; she also learned how to use the X-ray equipment itself. With the help of a military doctor and Irène, now a teenager, Curie made her first trip to the battlefront in the fall of 1914. If she could not help her native country just now, she was determined to pour all of her energies into serving her adopted country.

Marie also began collecting radon, the radioactive gas emitted by radium. She sealed the radon into glass tubes and had them delivered to military and civilian hospitals for use in treating diseased tissues in patients. With the award money from her second Nobel Prize, she invested in French war bonds. She even offered her Nobel medals to be melted down and used for the war effort, but officials at the Bank of France refused to destroy them.

Scientists were still unaware of the consequences of excessive exposure to X-rays at the time. Marie and Irène were constantly exposed to the dangers of the very radiation that saved the lives of countless soldiers. She insisted that the female volunteers who assisted with radiology— "manipulatrices," as they were later called—needed to be resourceful and inventive to solve the problems that confronted them when using the new technology in field hospitals. She opened her school for manipulatrices in October 1916 at a new training hospital in Paris, teaching women from all walks of life in intensive six-week courses. Between its opening and the end of the war in 1918, the school turned out 150 manipulatrices who were immediately shipped to assignments at mobile units and the more than 200 stationary facilities that Marie had set up throughout France.

All this might have been a bit easier had Marie not been forced to struggle against government officials who had no understanding of what X-rays could do and who were opposed to women being directly involved in the war effort. Further, many military officials did not believe it was proper to allow civilian workers to operate within a war zone independent of the army. Despite such opposition and in spite of her chronically poor health, Marie devoted herself to this new challenge with fervor and enthusiasm. Her expense records from that period are filled with notations of charitable donations to various organizations, including aid to Poland, aid to France, donations to soldiers themselves,

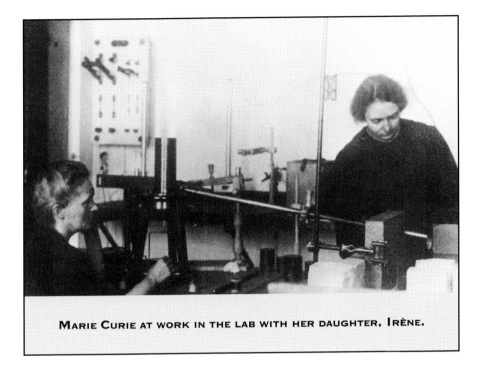

MARIE CURIE AT WORK IN THE LAB WITH HER DAUGHTER, IRÈNE.

to shelters for the poor, and even expenses cited as "yarn for soldiers" (she was most likely knitting garments for the troops).

Irène also helped her mother, eventually becoming a trainer of manipulatrices herself. At the beginning of the war, she impatiently waited at a vacation home in Brittany until she could be as useful as her mother in the war effort. In early September she wrote Marie about her frustrations and fear in staying with a Polish governess and housekeeper, which excited the suspicions of nearby residents. They apparently believed that the two were Germans and should immediately leave the country. Because Irène was staying with them, they accused her of being a German sympathizer. Marie understood very well her daughter's dilemma and her disappointment at being thought "less than French." She replied warmly:

> I was so sorry to hear that you have had some unpleas-antness about your nationality. Don't take these things too much to heart, but do your best to clarify things to people with whom you do business. Remember also that, not only should you endure these little problems with patience, but that it is in fact your duty to protect Josephine and Valentine [the housekeeper and governess]. . . . This would be your duty even if they were Germans, because . . . they would still have the right to visit in Brittany. *Chérie*, be more aware of exactly what your duty is, as a Frenchwoman, to yourself and to others.[4]

In early October, Irène and Eve returned home. Eve attended primary school, and Irène enrolled at the Sorbonne. A brilliant scholar in her own right, she earned her degree from the Sorbonne in math, physics, and chemistry. Irène ultimately joined her mother in the war effort. "Thrilled to be no longer considered a child, [Irène] thoroughly justified her mother's confidence. Irène's baptism of fire quickly matured her and tightened the bonds with Marie, who soon accepted her as an equal."[5] After the war, Irène earned an official appointment in her mother's laboratory. Their collaboration continued for the rest of Marie Curie's life. Irène herself would win the Nobel Prize in chemistry in 1935, with her husband, Frédéric Joliot.

By the time World War I ended, 1,375,800 French soldiers were dead. France, said Marie, "lost the elite of its youth."[6] With Germany, Britain, Russia, Austria-Hungary, and the other countries involved in the war, the loss of life was staggering. Almost 9 million died in combat and nearly 20 million total as a direct or indirect result of the war. On November 11, 1918, news that the armistice had been signed threw France into a massive victory celebration that lasted for days. Marie Curie heard the news while working in her lab, and she immediately went out in search of a flag of France. When none were available, she bought red, white, and blue material and made her own, hanging it triumphantly from the windows of the Radium Institute.

After the war, Marie began offering courses in radiology to American soldiers who were staying in France until they received orders to return home. She wrote a book, *Radiology in War*, about her experiences with the new science during World War I. By the fall of 1919, the Radium Institute was back up and running full-time. Marie spent the remainder of her years devoting her time to the Institute and her research.

One result of the Treaty of Versailles, which officially ended the war in 1919, was that Poland became an independent country for the first time in 123 years. That fact, along with the bitter experiences of World War I, changed Marie's political perspective forever. When it began, she had harbored a firm conviction that knowledge—in particular scientific knowledge—was the key to wisdom. Yet in the aftermath of the war, she was stunned to learn that a group of German scientists decided to support the autocratic Kaiser by signing what was called the Manifesto of the Ninety-Three, in which German intellectuals insisted that a German victory was the only means to advance civilization and promote the human race. When a friend asked Marie Curie to join intellectuals around the world in signing a document against war, she refused, saying that his views were "not entirely the same" as hers. "Certainly," she admitted, "I have a horror of war and I deplore, like you, the subjection of intelligence to brute force." But she added:

[T]he highest cultivation of intellect is not a guarantee of a just view of national and social problems. . . . Men whose minds deal in abstractions on the highest level and who produce admirable work have shown that they are ready to side with all kinds of acts of banditry committed on behalf of their country. A scholar who signs the Manifesto of the Ninety-three is humanly more remote from me than a simple citizen who is capable of seeking justice not only for himself but for others.[7]

Although she disagreed in principle with the signing of mass documents by academics and scientists, Marie nevertheless had discarded her belief that one could create a better world solely through devotion to science. In a letter she wrote to a friend, Marie confessed that she had yet to figure out how her participation in social activism would take hold, though she already understood that she felt more comfortable within the confines of a small homogenous group of individuals who all knew each other. Marie knew that in the group dynamic environment, all would examine a question thoroughly and form a substantive collective opinion about it.

Marie found just such a group in the League of Nations' Commission on Intellectual Cooperation. For more than twelve years, she devoted a great deal of energy to the commission's aim of encouraging and protecting the sharing of scientific knowledge, regardless of international borders and political regimes. Among the issues she promoted most

NORWAY

SWEDEN

FINLAND

UNION
OF
SOVIET
SOCIALIST
REPUBLICS

ESTONIA

LATVIA

DEN-
MARK

BALTIC
SEA

LITHUANIA

GREAT
BRITAIN

NETHER-
LANDS

GERMANY

• Warsaw

POLAND

BELGIUM

• Paris

CZECHOSLOVAKIA

FRANCE

SWITZ.

AUSTRIA

HUNGARY

RUMANIA

BLACK
SEA

YUGOSLAVIA

ITALY

BULGARIA

SPAIN

ALBANIA

GREECE

TURKEY

MEDITERRANEAN SEA

1918

THE BOUNDARIES OF EUROPE AS THEY WERE DIVIDED AT THE END OF WORLD WAR I IN 1918

fervently in the Commission was the question of scientific ownership and the rights of the individual scientist to his research and results. Although years earlier, she herself had renounced any form of patent on radium, she lobbied tirelessly for a means by which governments would reward individuals who freely gave their work to improve and benefit society. Marie was also instrumental in establishing an international bibliography of scientific publications and the development of guidelines for international scholarships in scientific pursuits.

Among those whom she convinced to join the Commission was Albert Einstein, who as a native German had refused to sign the Manifesto of the Ninety-three. Einstein at first accepted the invitation, believing that he and Madame Curie were of like mind on the issues promoted by the Commission. However, shortly after he accepted, a wealthy Jewish industrialist in Germany, Walther Rathenau, was assassinated after having been named foreign minister in the Weimar government. Einstein believed that the assassination was an ominous sign of what would soon become rabid anti-Semitism in Germany, and he wrote Marie Curie that he could not serve on such a committee. Einstein explained, "that he was resigning not only because of the murder of Rathenau, but because of anti-Semitism in Berlin and his feeling that he was 'no longer the right person for the job.'"[8] In spite of Marie's great disappointment and arguing that it was exactly for that reason that his presence was needed, Einstein continued to refuse to serve. Ultimately, the two scientists remained friends, although they occasionally differed on the role of the scientist in international relations.

CHAPTER EIGHT

A PERMANENT TRIBUTE TO PIERRE

Marie Curie hoped that the Radium Institute, now considered a world-class scientific facility, would serve as a lasting memorial to her husband, Pierre, and to his work. With assistance and contributions from such benefactors as French philanthropist Henri de Rothschild and American journalist Marie Meloney, the Radium Institute lived up to its reputation.

Mrs. Meloney, known to friends as "Missy," was instrumental in helping Marie establish the Marie Curie Radium Campaign, launched in an effort to secure additional radium for research purposes. Marie herself had just one gram of radium at the Institute; her plans for the research facility demanded that she find a way to secure more. She first met Missy Meloney in May 1920 when the latter was brought into the waiting room at the Institute and introduced as Mrs. William Brown Meloney, editor of a well-known New York magazine. Marie Curie saw a small, fragile-seeming woman with a slight limp from a childhood mishap, with gray hair and large black eyes. Marie Curie was the reporter's idol, and Missy had attempted several times before—without success—to arrange an interview with her. Finally, she wrote one last heartfelt letter to Curie, in which she explained, "My father, who was a medical man, used to say that it was impossible to exaggerate the unimportance of people. But you have been important to me for twenty years, and I want to see you a few minutes."[1] Marie Curie finally agreed.

Missy Meloney was so thrilled to meet her idol that at first she was unable to speak. Marie put her at ease by beginning the conversation. "America has about fifty grams of radium," she declared. "Four of these are in Baltimore, six in Denver, seven in New York." After Marie finished naming other U.S. locations of radium, Missy asked, "And in France?" "My laboratory has hardly more than a gram."[2] Missy was stunned—not only did the great Marie Curie, and the entire country of France, have access only to one gram of radium, but the radium was not even owned by Marie; it belonged to the Institute. The reporter also learned that the market price of a single gram of radium was about $100,000 in U.S. currency. It was easy to see why the Radium Institute was struggling: although housed in a new building, the facility did not have enough equipment, and what little it had was not up-to-date. Additionally, the radium held there was used only to extract emanation for hospital use in treating cancer. When asked what she would most like to have, Marie Curie answered simply, "I need a gram of radium to continue my researches, but I cannot buy it: radium is too dear for me."[3]

Thus was launched Missy Meloney's plan to secure for Marie Curie a gram of radium. Upon her return to America, she unsuccessfully sought donations of $10,000 each from 10 wealthy patronesses to fund the purchase. Only three women agreed. Undeterred, she abandoned that plan for another in which she created a committee whose members would launch a national campaign—the Marie Curie Radium Campaign—to solicit donations from all women. As an added incentive to potential donors and as a favor to the committee members, Marie Curie ultimately agreed to travel to the United States. She departed France via ocean liner in early May 1921, accompanied by her daughters and Mrs. Meloney, who had returned to France to escort her. By that time, Missy Meloney had already secured the $100,000 required to purchase the gram of radium.

For most of the trip, Marie sequestered herself in order to avoid well-wishers, photographers, and reporters. The reverence and enthusiasm with which Marie was received in the United States both surprised and frightened her. She had long suffered from frequent bouts of weakness and poor health, but during her seven-week stay in America, she deteriorated even further. Several months before, she had begun experiencing a continuous humming in her ears that gradually worsened. Even more worrisome was that her eyes had begun to fail rapidly. At a farewell celebration at the opera in Paris before she left for America, she could not even see clearly what was happening on stage. She hid her failing health from all but her family and closest friends. It seemed that she was finally beginning to realize that perhaps her work with radium was responsible for the many physical problems she had endured.

Among the dignitaries Marie met while in the United States was President Warren G. Harding, who presented her with the gram of radium during a special White House ceremony. She received 10 honorary degrees from colleges and universities, and numerous medals and honorary memberships; she also sat through scores of luncheons, dinners, and meetings. The hectic pace took its toll. Despite the warmth of her American reception, she was famously described in the *Kansas City Post* on May 19 as seeming "Shy, Weary, and Disinterested" during one particular reception in her honor.[4]

Still, Marie Curie could not be swayed from her prime objective in coming to America. She made sure that Missy Meloney found a lawyer to help her process the deed of a gift of radium. Marie wanted to be certain that the radium given to her was "for free and untrammeled use by her in experimentation and in pursuit of knowledge"[5] and would immediately become the property of her laboratory. She had no intention of wrangling over ownership of the precious gram of radium.

The Curies boarded a ship for the return to France on June 25, 1921, carrying not only the precious additional gram of radium, but also vital ores, costly lab equipment, and cash for her institute. The tour had been difficult and extremely strenuous, but Marie came away with an encouraging sense of the "unlimited possibilities for the future" in America.[6] She had also contracted to write an autobiography for an American publisher, which would provide additional income in the form of royalties. Most important, Marie

Curie had established contacts and secured resources that would allow her to continue—and expand—her own work for years to come.

In France, a new generation of scientists was taking hold. No longer was power wielded by older, more conservative organizations such as the Academy of Sciences. Marie Curie's institute had been receiving private grants for many years, and along with the Pasteur Institute, it had set a new standard for scientific research outside of academics. With the aid of scientific leaders such as Jean Perrin and the financial backing of the Rockefeller Foundation, the Rothschild Foundation, and others, a new group of scientific institutes began to spring up along the rue Pierre Curie, near the Radium Institute. Curie and a number of her colleagues created the Curie Foundation, with the mission of providing both the scientific and the medical divisions of the Radium Institute with adequate resources. Over the next two decades the Curie Foundation became a major international force in the treatment of cancer.

Marie Curie traveled once more to the United States to meet with President Hoover in 1929; again, the tour was arranged by Missy Meloney. On this trip, she was equally as successful as she had been in 1921: with the support she received she was able to fully equip the Warsaw Radium Institute in Poland, which she had co-founded with her sister Bronya, who became its director. This second Institute became an international center for the study of radioactivity.

Now that Marie spent most of her time and energy on directing the Institute in Paris, she no longer had large blocks of time to devote to her own research. The scientists and researchers who worked at the Institute thrived,

MARIE CURIE AT WORK IN THE LAB, ALONE, CIRCA 1920. CURIE REMAINED
A TIRELESS WORKER THROUGHOUT HER LIFE.

however. For example, Salomon Rosenblum helped to confirm quantum theory through his work at the Institute with actinium. Irène Curie and her husband, Frédéric Joliot, earned the 1935 Nobel Prize for chemistry.

By the 1930s it had become very clear that work Marie and Pierre had accomplished with radium had most likely been responsible for Pierre's poor health, and had now left Marie permanently debilitated. Nor could she—or other scientists working with radioactivity—deny that other lab workers were also suffering from the deadly effects of radiation. The realization came slowly, in part because radiation's effects were unseen and stealthy, and the symptoms of radiation poisoning differed from person to person. Clues about the dangers of radiation were evident in the fact that it was able to cure certain cancerous tissues by destroying malignant cells, but in the minds of early 20th-century scientists, nearly all scientific discoveries were viewed as progress and therefore as entirely beneficial.

The first official inkling of the deadly nature of radioactivity had come from the United States, which had reported in 1925 that several painters of luminous watch dials in a New Jersey plant had either died or suffered from irreversible diseases such as anemia and deterioration of the jaw. That year, Marie mourned the loss of two laboratory workers who died within four days of each other after preparing thorium X for medical use in a small Paris factory.

Years later, Marie herself struggled to conceal her illness, not only from the public, but from others who worked in her lab. One reason was that she detested being pitied and refused to have anyone treat her as weak or helpless. Most important, however, was the fact that to admit her illness to herself was also to admit that she had to stop working. And she had no intention of doing so. "Sometimes my courage fails me and I think I ought to stop working, live in the country and devote myself to gardening," she wrote Bronya in September 1927. "But I am held by a thousand bonds. . . . Nor do I know whether, even by writing scientific books, I could live without the laboratory."[7]

Marie's later years were nevertheless filled with triumphs and sadness. In 1930 she heard that Jacques Curie was very ill, and she rushed to his home in Montpellier to attend to him, despite her own weak health. Later, when she heard the awful news that her niece, Bronya's daughter, had died in the United States, an apparent victim of suicide, she was devastated. She began to miss her family in Poland more keenly, even as it grew smaller. She began taking more frequent vacations, to Cavalaire in winter and to Britanny in the summer, where her daughters taught her how to swim. In 1926 Irène, at twenty-nine, married another scientist named Frédéric Joliot, and Marie joyfully greeted her first grandchildren, Hélène and Pierre, named after his grandfather.

> *"Nor do I know whether, even by writing scientific books, I could live without the laboratory."*
>
> **—Marie Curie**

Perhaps equally exciting to Marie Curie were the discoveries that her daughter and son-in-law were making in the laboratory. With Ernest Rutherford, they were instrumental in experiments that led James Chadwick, of Rutherford's laboratory, to discover the neutron. In 1932, the Joliot-Curies had published a paper that built on the work of Walther Bothe and Herbert Becker, who had bombarded light elements with alpha particles from polonium and discovered that beryllium, when subjected to the rays, produced a radiation stronger than the bombarding particles. Irène and Fréderic's paper demonstrated that the radiation from the beryllium was knocking protons out of the hydrogen. They also concluded that they were creating unstable, "radioactive" isotopes of elements—isotopes that did not exist naturally and that decayed over time to form another element. The ramifications of the discovery were enormous.

The Joliot-Curies made the discovery on January 15, 1934. Fréderic excitedly called his good friend Pierre Biquard and asked him to come to the lab and witness what he and his wife had discovered. While he was demonstrating, Marie Curie and Paul Langevin entered the room. "I will never forget the expression of intense joy which overtook [Marie Curie] when Irène and I showed her the first [artificially produced] radioactive element in a little glass tube," Fréderic later remembered. "I can see her still taking this little tube of the radioelement, already quite weak, in her radium-damaged fingers. To verify what we were telling her, she brought the Geiger-Muller counter up close to it and she could hear the numerous clicks. . . . This was without a doubt the last great satisfaction of her life."[8]

Marie Curie's health continued to decline, and on July 4, seven months after that exciting day, she died. After her death, doctors were finally able to diagnose what they could not while she was living: her cause of death was attributed to "aplastic pernicious anemia of rapid, feverish development."[9] Anemia, a condition of the blood that prevents oxygen absorption and causes intense fatigue, can usually be corrected by the body's bone marrow, which produces new red blood cells. But in Marie's case, even her bone marrow had been damaged by radiation exposure, and it was unable to combat the anemia. Even in death, Marie was able to provide valuable information to medical practitioners and scientists—information that helped to avert further harm to other researchers of radioactivity.

Marie Curie was interred twice: after her death, she was laid to rest next to her beloved Pierre in the small cemetery in Sceaux. Her family traveled to the funeral carrying small containers of Polish soil to sprinkle on her coffin. Sixty years after Marie's death, her remains and those of Pierre were reinterred in France's national mausoleum, the Panthéon—the resting place of honor for the most eminent French citizens.

ACTIVITIES

Learning the Periodic Table of Elements

Pierre & Marie Curie discovered new elements in their research. Go to your local library, or search the web to locate the Periodic Table of Elements chart. Many of these elements are so common they can be found in and around your environment, in the things we own and even in the foods we eat. See how many of the elements from the Periodic Table you can find in your own surroundings.

For example: The element symbol AU (#79) stands for the metal gold. Can you find something made of gold?

Observing the Decay of Molecules

Radioactive materials decay. Because of their harmful radioactivity, these kinds of materials cannot be handled freely. However, to understand the concept of molecule decay, you can observe the process by buying a simple "glow stick" from your local novelty store.

Glow sticks, often called light sticks, use energy from a chemical reaction to emit light. The chemical reaction is set off by mixing multiple chemical compounds. The reaction causes a substantial release of energy.

Snapping the glow stick mixes the chemicals inside the tube, releasing energy that emits light. However, after a period of time the chemical reaction stops and eventually the glow stick no longer emits light. It is the decay of the molecules that ends the process because they lose their energy. Radioactive atoms behave in the same way. When the molecules decay, the radioactive atoms become "non-radioactive."

CHRONOLOGY

1867—Marie Salomée Skłodowska is born near Warsaw, Poland, on November 7.

1876—Sister Zosia dies.

1878—Bronisława Boguska Skłodowski, Marie's mother, dies of tuberculosis.

1883—Graduates from Madame Jadwiga Sikorska private school.

1886—To help sister Bronya attend medical school in Paris, Marie becomes a governess.

1889—After four years as a governess, Marie moves back home.

1891—At age twenty-three, Marie moves to Paris and enrolls at the Sorbonne.

1893—Marie ranks first among those taking the *licence és sciences* exam.

1894—Marie ranks second among those taking the *licence ès mathèmatiques* exam.

1895—Marie marries Pierre Curie on July 26.

1897—Marie gives birth to her first child, Irène, on September 12.

1898—Marie and Pierre discover two new elements, polonium and radium.

1903—Marie earns her Ph.D. in physics, June 25.

Pierre, Marie, and Henri Becquerel are awarded the Nobel Prize in Physics for their research on radioactivity.

1904—Marie gives birth to her second child, Eve, on December 6.

1906—While trying to cross the street on April 19, Pierre Curie is run over and killed by a horse-drawn carriage.
Marie assumes Pierre's professorship at the Sorbonne, becoming the first woman to teach there.

1910—Isolates radium; publishes her course as *Traité de radioactivité* (Treatise on Radioactivity).

1911—Fails to be elected to the Academy of Sciences.
Attends first Solvay Conference as the only woman among such notable scientists as Poincaré, Einstein, Planck, and Rutherford.
The Royal Swedish Academy of Sciences awards Marie the Nobel Prize in Chemistry for her success in isolating radium.
At the request of an International Commission, establishes an international standard for radium; the unit is the curie.

1912—Building of Radium Institute is begun. One building will house Marie Curie's laboratory devoted to the physics and chemistry of radioactivity, and the second, headed by Dr. Claudius Regaud, for the investigation of medical applications.

1914—Radium Institute open in Paris, France, with Marie as its first director.

1914–1918—World War I begins on August 4. Organizes radiological services in wartime hospitals; outfits X-ray cars; teaches radiological technicians.

1919—Radium Institute is now fully open. Marie Curie's laboratory flourishes in the 1920s and 1930s.

1921—With Irène and Eve, tours America at the invitation of journalist Missy Meloney; accepts a gram of radium from the President of the United States; attends Yale commencement where she receives an honorary Yale Doctorate of Science.

1925—Irène Curie obtains her doctorate in science based on work done in her mother's laboratory.

1926—Irène Curie marries Frédéric Joliot, who is carrying out research for his doctoral degree in Marie Curie's laboratory.

1929—Second tour of America; receives the gift of a gram of radium for the Radium Institute in Warsaw.

1934—Dies July 4 of aplastic pernicious anemia.

1935—Irène Joliot-Curie and Frédéric Joliot win the Nobel Prize in Chemistry for artificial radioactivity. Ensures the publication of Marie Curie's textbook, *Radioactivité*, based on her lectures, that she completed just before she died.

1937—Eve Curie publishes *Madame Curie*, one of the most widely read scientific biographies of all time.

CHAPTER NOTES

Chapter One: A First for the Nobel Academy

1. Eve Curie, *Madame Curie* (New York: Da Capo Press, Inc., 1986), p. 279.

2. "Marie Curie—Scandal and Recovery (1910–1913)," *American Institute of Physics*, n.d., <http://www.aip.org/history/curie/scandal1.htm> (March 9, 2004).

3. Rosalynd Pflaum, *Grand Obsession: Marie Curie and Her World* (New York: Doubleday, 1989), p. 160.

4. Ibid., p. 164.

5. Ibid., p. 164.

6. Ibid., p. 165.

7. "The Nobel Prize in Chemistry 1911," *Nobel e-Museum*, June 23, 2003, <http://www.nobel.se/chemistry/laureates/1911/index.html> (March 9, 2004).

8. "Marie Curie—Nobel Lecture," *Nobel e-Museum*, August 29, 2003, <http://www.nobel.se/chemistry/laureates/1911/marie-curie-lecture.html> (March 9, 2004).

9. Ibid.

10. Ibid.

Chapter Two: Oppression and Tragedy in Poland

1. Susan Quinn, *Marie Curie: A Life* (New York: Simon and Schuster, 1995), p. 27.

2. Eve Curie, *Madame Curie* (New York: Da Capo Press, Inc., 1986), p. 13.

3. Rosalynd Pflaum, *Grand Obsession: Marie Curie and Her World* (New York: Doubleday, 1989), p. 5.

4. Ibid., p. 5.

5. Quinn, p. 41.

6. Curie, p. 32.

7. Quinn, p. 47.

Chapter Three: The Long Road to Paris

1. Eve Curie, *Madame Curie* (New York: Da Capo Press, Inc., 1986), p. 40

2. Susan Quinn, *Marie Curie: A Life* (New York: Simon and Schuster, 1995), p. 56.

3. Ibid., p. 59.

4. Ibid., p. 61.

5. Rosalynd Pflaum, *Grand Obsession: Marie Curie and Her World* (New York: Doubleday, 1989), p. 13.

6. Ibid., p. 12.

7. Curie, pp. 53–54.

8. Ibid., pp. 72–73.

9. Ibid., p. 73.

10. Ibid., p. 86.

11. Quinn, p. 89.

12. Ibid., p. 91.

13. Ibid., p. 99.

Chapter Four: Research Leads to Discovery

1. Susan Quinn, *Marie Curie: A Life* (New York: Simon and Schuster, 1995), p. 104.

2. Ibid., p. 106.

3. Ibid., p. 109.

4. Ibid., p.112.

5. Eve Curie, *Madame Curie* (New York: Da Capo Press, Inc., 1986), p. 124.

6. Ibid., p.127.

7. "Marie Curie—A Student in Paris (1891–1897)," *American Institute of Physics*, n.d., <http://www.aip.org/history/curie/stud2.htm> (March 9, 2004).

8. Ibid.

Chapter Five: A Path Shaped Out of Tragedy

1. Susan Quinn, *Marie Curie: A Life* (New York: Simon and Schuster, 1995), p. 197.

2. Ibid., p. 198.

3. Ibid., p. 213.

4. Ibid., p. 214.

5. Eve Curie, *Madame Curie* (New York: Da Capo Press, Inc., 1986), p. 226.

6. Ibid., p. 235

7. Ibid., p. 227.

8. Ibid., p. 227.

9. Ibid., pp. 227–28.

10. "Marie Curie—Tragedy and Adjustment (1906–1910)," *American Institute of Physics*, n.d., <http://www.aip.org/history/curie/trag1.htm> (March 9, 2004).

11. Curie, p. 247.

12. Ibid., p. 249.

13. "Marie Curie—Tragedy and Adjustment (1906–1910)."

14. Curie, p. 254.

15. Ibid.

Chapter Six: Harsh Judgment And Renewal

1. Susan Quinn, *Marie Curie: A Life* (New York: Simon and Schuster, 1995), p. 260.

2. Rosalynd Pflaum, *Grand Obsession: Marie Curie and Her World* (New York: Doubleday, 1989), p. 154.

3. Quinn, p. 278.

4. Ibid., p. 279.

5. Eve Curie, *Madame Curie* (New York: Da Capo Press, Inc., 1986), p. 278.

6. Quinn, p. 302.

7. Pflaum, p. 164.

8. Quinn, p. 307.

9. Curie, p. 281.

10. Ibid., p. 282.

Chapter Seven: Innovation at the Battlefront

1. Susan Quinn, *Marie Curie: A Life* (New York: Simon and Schuster, 1995), p. 355.

2. Rosalynd Pflaum, *Grand Obsession: Marie Curie and Her World* (New York: Doubleday, 1989), p. 194.

3. Eve Curie, *Madame Curie* (New York: Da Capo Press, Inc., 1986), p. 290.

4. Quinn, pp. 368–369.

5. Pflaum, p. 200.

6. Quinn, p. 374.

7. Ibid., pp. 378–79.

8. Ronald W. Clark, *Einstein: The Life and Times* (New York: Avon Books, 1972), p. 431.

Chapter Eight: A Permanent Tribute to Pierre

1. Eve Curie, *Madame Curie* (New York: Da Capo Press, Inc., 1986), p. 322.

2. Ibid., p. 323.

3. Ibid., p. 324.

4. Reid, Robert. *Marie Curie*. New York: E.P. Dutton & Co., 1974, p. 263.

5. Ibid., p. 263.

6. Susan Quinn, *Marie Curie: A Life* (New York: Simon and Schuster, 1995), p. 339.

7. Ibid., p. 417.

8. Ibid., p. 430.

9. Ibid., pp. 431–32.

GLOSSARY

actinium—Radioactive metallic element found especially in pitchblende (a brownish-black mineral that is a source of uranium and radium).

anemia—A condition in which the blood has less than the normal amount of red blood cells, hemoglobin, or total volume.

anti-Semitism—Hostility toward or discrimination against Jews as a religious, ethnic, or racial group.

atomic—Relating to or concerned with atoms, atomic energy, or atom bombs.

autocrat—A person who rules with unlimited authority.

barium—A silver-white poisonous metallic element that occurs only in combination with other elements.

beryllium—A steel-gray, light, strong, and brittle toxic metallic element used chiefly to help harden alloys.

bismuth—A heavy brittle grayish-white metallic element that is chemically like arsenic and antimony.

bone marrow—A soft tissue, rich in fat and blood vessels, that fills the cavities of most bones.

crystal—A solid form of a substance that has a regularly repeating internal arrangement of its atoms and often external flat faces (as a snowflake crystal).

curie—A unit of radioactivity equal to 37 billion disintegrations per second.

delegation—One or more persons chosen to represent others or to represent a government or nation.

doctorate—The degree, title, or rank of a doctor.

emancipation—The act or process of making free.

hypothesis—Something not proved but assumed to be true for purposes of argument or further study.

insurgent—A person who revolts against civil authority or an established government; especially one who is not recognized as hostile.

intellectual—One who is given to study, reflection, and speculation; a person engaged in activity requiring the creative use of the intellect.

isotope—Any of two or more types of atoms of the same chemical element that have the same atomic number and nearly identical chemical behavior but have different atomic masses and different physical properties.

lorry—A large, open truck or cart.

nationalism—Loyalty and devotion to a nation, especially when expressed as a glorifying of one nation above all others and an emphasis on its culture and interests.

pension—A sum paid regularly to a person, especially after retirement.

philanthropist—One who practices goodwill to others or makes an active effort to promote human welfare.

physicist—One who specializes in the science that deals with matter and energy and their interactions.

polonium—A radioactive metallic element that is similar to tellurium and bismuth and found especially in pitchblende (a brownish-black mineral that is a source of uranium and radium).

positivism—A theory that positive knowledge is based on

natural phenomena and their properties and relations, as they can be proved by science.

quantum theory—A theory in physics based on the idea that radiant energy (as light) is composed of small separate packets of energy.

radioactivity—The giving off of rays of energy or particles by the breaking apart of atoms of certain elements (such as uranium).

radium—A strongly radioactive shining white metallic element that occurs in combination in very small quantities in minerals; radium is used in treating cancer.

radon—A heavy radioactive gaseous element formed when radium atoms break apart.

spiritism—The view that spirit is a prime element of reality; also called spiritualism.

symmetry—Close agreement in size, shape, and position of parts arranged on opposite sides of a dividing line or plane or around a central point.

uranium—A silvery, heavy, radioactive metallic element that exists naturally as a mixture of three forms with different atomic mass numbers: 234, 235, and 238.

utilitarian—Of or relating to usefulness.

X-ray—An electromagnetic radiation that is produced by bombarding a metallic target with fast electrons in vacuum and that is able to penetrate various thicknesses of solids and to act on photographic film similarly to light.

FURTHER READING

Birch, Beverly. *Marie Curie: Courageous Pioneer in the Study of Radioactivity*. Farmington Hills, Mich.: Gale Group, 2000.

Hasday, Judy. *Albert Einstein: The Giant of 20th Century Science*. Berkeley Heights, N.J.: Enslow Publishers, Inc., 2004.

Parker, Steve. *Marie Curie and Radium*. Broomall, Pa.: Chelsea House, 1995.

Lassieur, Allison. *Marie Curie: A Scientific Pioneer.* Danbury, Conn.: Franklin Watts, Inc., 2003.

Waxman, Laura Hamilton. *Marie Curie*. Minneapolis, Minn.: Lerner Publications Company, 2003.

INTERNET ADDRESSES

Marie Curie and the History of Radioactivity
http://www.sciencemuseum.org.uk/on-line/curie/index.asp

Nobel e-Museum
http://www.nobel.se/chemistry/laureates/1911/marie-curie-bio.html

Timelinescience: Marie Curie and the Discovery of Radium
http://www.timelinescience.org/resource/students/curie/curie.htm

INDEX